Business's
Most Wanted

Business's Most Wanted

Most Wanted

The Top 10 Book of Corporate
Greed, Eccentric Entrepreneurs,
and Management Oddities

Jim Romeo

Potomac Books, Inc.
Washington, D.C.

Library of Congress Cataloging-in-Publication Data

Romeo, Jim, 1961–
    Business's most wanted : the top 10 book of
corporate greed, eccentric entrepreneurs, and
management
oddities / Jim Romeo.—1st ed.
        p. cm.
    Includes bibliographical references and index.
    ISBN 1-57488-661-4 (alk. paper)
    1. Businesspeople—United States—Biography.
    2. Business enterprises—United States—History.
    3. Business—United States—Miscellanea.   I. Title.
HC102.5.A2R66 2004
388.092'273—dc22   2004010786

Printed in Canada on acid-free paper that
meets the American National Standards
Institute Z39-48 Standard.

Potomac Books, Inc.
22841 Quicksilver Drive
Dulles, Virginia 20166

First Edition

10 9 8 7 6 5 4 3 2 1

Contents

THE PRODUCTS

THE CLIMATE

Illustrations

Introduction

The business of America is business. Calvin Coolidge said it. And I believe it.

The shoes you wear; the keyboard on which you click; the health care you receive; the credit cards you use; the automobile you drive—they're all linked to our Gross National Product and the many products and services that go out the door every day of the week. The things that go into making and managing these products and services make up the landscape of American enterprise. It is serious business.

The lists found in this book are organized along the same lines that a businessperson would consider: the people, the products, and the climate. All three are present in almost every business scenario.

Firms produce products and services. Products and services are bought, sold, and exchanged against many different climates. They are influenced by a wide variety of people—consumers, middle managers, chief executives, economists, and many others. The myriad interactions of business provide an entertaining and interesting stage.

This stage is filled with facts, figures, and other oddities that are interesting to explore and know about. In fact, it would make a good book. And so it has. What's peculiar about this book is that it takes a serious topic and makes it not so serious.

A trivia book takes what some may view as extraordinary facts of their serious business and makes them ordinary, trivial, and entertaining. Common knowledge isn't nearly as entertaining as are little-known facts. Microsoft's mission statement is far more boring than the layout of Bill Gates's house. An understanding of the strength of the U.S. economy isn't as entertaining as reading about how our public debt has skyrocketed since the 1960s. Business trivia always seems to be a better read than ordinary business facts and figures.

This book is an attempt to uncover business trivia that entertains and at the same time informs. It is a break from the serious side of business and the stuffed-shirt stereotype.

Another valuable part of this book is the power of ten. Trivia is more entertaining when grouped in bunches of ten. Ten commonalities make a subject more interesting. A secretary of the treasury from New York isn't so interesting until you find out there are at least nine others who have a strong New York connection. A great innovation isn't as interesting as ten great innovations. To know that one particular chief executive was at one time a White House Fellow isn't as interesting to know as the fact that there are at least ten notable leaders in business who were also White House Fellows.

This book also demonstrates how business trivia helps us appreciate history. Historically there have always been philanthropists, con artists, and innovators. Read some of the lists in the book and you'll soon discover that history really does repeat itself. Business trivia helps us understand historical trends: the quest for fair labor and working conditions, our capitalist convictions, the rise and fall of great business leaders, and the fascinating backgrounds that have surrounded famous entrepreneurs and business leaders for centuries. In trivia, there is much history.

The book is organized in such a way that you don't have to read it from cover to cover. You can bounce to areas that interest you. You can explore a section about successful businesspeople who were card players and then flip to a list of business leaders who were former Eagle Scouts. If you feel like reading about finance one day, you can flip to that section with no worry about having missed something in an earlier chapter.

This book should also have a long shelf life. Many of its facts and figures and other oddities are from decades ago. These gems of information were amusing in the past and will continue to amuse in years to come. It will be interesting to see how the national debt measures up in the next decade after you see in this book how it has multiplied like an amoeba since the 1960s. It will also be interesting to see how we all talk about the bursting of the dot-com bubble in the years to come. And it will be interesting to see what future presidents have to say about entitlements in light of what has been said in the past, as this book points out.

I've discovered that the business world is so huge and encompasses so many avenues that it would take a string of books to fill all of these avenues of business. This book is a good start, and I sincerely hope you enjoy its content.

It's a big world out there, but the business of America certainly is business—in the purest sense of the word.

THE
PEOPLE

The Darkest Chambers of Industrial Society

The culture of the corporate rat race has always been characterized by gut-wrenching, dog-eat-dog competitive spirit and a survival-of-the-fittest credo. Thus it may be fitting that many leaders and shapers of industry have suffered from mental illness. And in fact, while this may be true, it wasn't easy finding out who they were, as it is certainly a private matter. Here are some well-known business leaders who have been forward with their illness, or who sadly fell victim to the silent suffering of a mental illness.

1. PHILIP GRAHAM (1915–1963)

Graham was the former chairman of the *Washington Post.* In 1963 Graham committed suicide after struggling with manic depression. His wife, Katherine, took over as publisher of the paper from 1969 to 1979 and was actively involved in its operation until her death in 2001.

2. TED TURNER (1938–   )

Turner is the founder and head of Turner Broadcasting. Despite his hotshot, happy-go-lucky demeanor, Turner fell victim to mental illness in 1985. He was treated for manic depression and took lithium for years. The accomplishments of Turner, who always gives the appearance of a no-nonsense business titan, have been overshadowed by his arrogance. Despite his haughty demeanor and his admission of having bipolar affective disorder, this notable philanthropist reportedly made the largest single philanthropic donation, of $1 billion, to the United Nations for its "good works" program.

3.   HEINZ PRECHTER (1942-2001)

A German immigrant, Prechter was the chairman of ASC Inc. (American Sunroof Corporation), a large auto supplier. Prechter suffered from severe bouts of manic depression. He was a friend of and major donor to President George W. Bush. He was most discreet about his illness and, sadly, committed suicide at age fifty-nine.

4.   PAUL GOTTLIEB (1935-2002)

Gottlieb was president and publisher of Harry N. Abrams, Inc. for over twenty years. Gottlieb suffered from depression that deepened even as his career took off. Like many others, he treated and managed his depression through medical care. He died from a heart attack in June 2002.

5.   ROBERT CAMPEAU (1924-   )

Campeau is a Canadian financier, real estate executive developer, and founder of Campeau Construction Company. Campeau launched a hostile takeover of Allied Stores Corporation, the United State's third largest retailer, in 1986 and acquired Federated Department Stores in 1988. He is a known manic-depressive and treats his illness through medical care.

6.   JOHN STUART MILL (1806-1873)

Mill helped shape much of the thinking and progress in nineteenth-century Britain with his essays on economics and philosophy, most famously his "On Liberty" in 1859. In 1826, at the age of twenty, he suffered from a nervous breakdown. He described his anxiety in the artful style of an essayist by saying, "I carried it with me into all companies, into all occupations."[1]

7. ROBERT MONDAVI (1913–   )

The winemaker and vineyard manager supposedly did not suffer from the more common mental illnesses such as anxiety or depression, but he did enter therapy when he was having emotional difficulty with his business pressures and family life. Allegedly, through therapy he was able to divert some of his focus away from his winery business and onto his family life.

8. HOWARD HUGHES (1905–1976)

Hughes was a film producer, an aviator, and the founder of Hughes Aircraft Corporation. Despite his many successes, he fell victim to obsessive-compulsive disorder (OCD), which led to his being one of the most well-known phobics. One of his phobias was microphobia—that is, he was fearful of germs. It is rumored that he used up boxes of tissues by wiping everything in sight. It's also rumored that he became agoraphobic—afraid of open spaces and unfamiliar places. He died on April 5, 1976, in a private jet as he was being flown to a hospital in Houston. The estate he left behind was estimated at $2 billion.

9. JOHN KENNETH GALBRAITH (1908–   )

Galbraith is an economist, educator, and author. The world-renowned economist was also a noted scholar and diplomat, with posts as a Harvard professor (1949–1975), U.S. ambassador to India (1961–1963), and personal advisor to President Kennedy. He is said to have suffered from unipolar disorder, whereby one's mood gravitates to either happy or sad. Unipolar disorder differs from bipolar disorder in that the

[1] Quote from http://www.healthyplace.com/communities/anxiety/paems/people/famous_people_2.htm.

mood swing is to one extreme or the other, but stays there rather than oscillating between the two as it does with bipolar disorder.

10. JAMES FORRESTAL (1892–1949)

Before he entered politics, Forrestal had earned a vast fortune as an investment banker. He later went on to become the undersecretary (1940) and then the secretary of the U.S. Navy (1944). He also became the first secretary of defense (1947–1949). Sadly, he took his life in 1949, convinced that he had failed the nation as secretary of defense. He is said to have suffered from severe depression.

Financial Name Droppers

So you want to hobnob with the high and mighty finance, banker, dollar-sign types, but you are fearful that you don't know the landscape? Here are some names you shouldn't leave home without knowing, as they make up a solid sampling of notable figures from the canyons of Wall Street.[1]

1. JOHN PIERPONT (J. P.) MORGAN (1837–1913)

One of the names most associated with Wall Street fame during the latter part of the nineteenth and beginning of the twentieth century, J. P. Morgan dominated the banking industry like no one before or since. In 1895 he made a significant profit from stopping a run on the U.S. Treasury's gold reserves, and in 1907 he headed a group of bankers who ended a financial panic by guaranteeing the solvency of weak banks. He also was one of the chief financiers and organizers in the railroad and steel industries, creating the massive U.S. Steel Corporation in 1901. He was on the other

[1] Information gathered from www.knowledgeproducts.net/walstreetits .html and www.ml.com.

John Pierpont (J. P.) Morgan, pictured here in 1873,
was America's foremost banker and financier from the late
nineteenth century until his death in 1913.

side of the trustbusters during Theodore Roosevelt's administration, when trusts controlled everything and big business
was large and tended toward being monopolistic.

2. WARREN BUFFET (1930–   )

Buffet took Benjamin Graham's and David Dodd's courses
in security analysis at Columbia University and went on to
become an independent investment entrepreneur during the
latter half of the twentieth century. He bought companies he
liked and could understand and holds on to them for dear
life. Buffet, who comes from Omaha, Nebraska, prides himself on his plain and simple ways combined with his savvy
investment intellect in the financial jungle. He is known to
many as "The Oracle of Omaha."

3. HETTY GREEN (1835–1916)

If you think that only men are market makers on Wall Street,
think again. Hetty Green was Wall Street's first female financier and said to be the richest woman in the world of her
day. Born in New Bedford, Massachusetts, her Quaker principles of thrift and prudence helped her turn a $6 million in-
heritance into $100 million. Because of her wealth, Green
feared she would wind up on the wrong end of an assassin's
bullet and indeed died from such a tragedy in 1916. She was
a major benefactor for Wellesley College and the Girl Scouts
of America.

4. DIAMOND JIM BRADY (1856–1917)

Brady was a larger-than-life figure of the 1890s and an example of a true rags-to-riches story. Brady began his career
as a hotel bellboy, but his super skills as a salesman turned
him into a world-class financier and philanthropist. His big
break resulted from his pioneering of scientific analysis to
help his employer, railroad supply firm Manning, Maxwell,
and Moore, anticipate and meet its clients' needs. Brady became almost obsessed with lavish diamond jewelry, hence

his name. A true fat cat, he had a huge appetite and was known to eat tremendous breakfasts, mid-morning snacks, and dinners that encompassed virtually the entire menu at the New York restaurants he frequented. Once, he went into a New England candy manufacturer and shoved off a check for $150,000 worth of candy, calling it the best candy he had ever eaten. This may have set the trend later for Warren Buffett, who bought See's Candy Company after he said it was the best candy *he* had ever eaten—an interesting parallel. Upon his death, much of his estate went to Johns Hopkins University Hospital and New York Hospital.

5.   JESSE LIVERMORE (1877–1940)

Known to many as the king of speculation, Livermore lived flamboyantly and was very garrulous about the fine craft of investing during the first half of the twentieth century. Livermore was known as "Boy Plunger," "the Great Bear," "the Wall Street Wonder," and "the Cotton King." Unlike many of his winning speculator counterparts, Livermore made millions, and subsequently lost millions, from his investments. He did this about four times during his thirty-year reign.

6.   BERNARD BARUCH (1870–1965)

By the time he was thirty, Bernard Baruch had made a fortune in the stock market. He served as a governor of the New York Stock Exchange and later became a presidential advisor. He later helped finance the Democratic Party and Democratic campaigns, including Woodrow Wilson's successful presidential campaign in 1912. His investing wisdom, he claimed, was going against the crowd—buying when others were selling and selling when others were buying. Say what you will, but it worked. However, the legend that Baruch shrewdly got out of the stock market before the crash of 1929 is not true. But since his fortune was not wiped out, he did fare better than many of his peers.

7. JOSEPH P. KENNEDY (1888-1969)

An entrepreneur and speculator, Kennedy built up a $500 million fortune and later headed the Securities and Exchange Commission. He made his money through investment banking, a chain of movie theaters, a film production company, New York real estate, and stock market investments. Perhaps his most infamous venture was a franchise on Scotch whiskey and British gin. Many say he wasn't of the same grain as his sons, who later went on to become some of the most recognizable and notable names in the early part of twentieth-century America, but he was nevertheless at the source of much of the Kennedy fortune.

8. GEORGE SOROS (1930-)

Born to a Jewish family in Budapest, Hungary, Soros made the trek from poor immigrant to billionaire. Soros has become the bellwether of investors and the envy of many of the titanic investors of the Wall Street age. He remains an ardent investor today.

9. CHARLES E. MERRILL (1885-1956) AND EDMUND C. LYNCH (1885-1952)

In 1907 Charles E. Merrill moved to New York City from Florida to work for a textile company. In the same city he found another person seeking a new adventure in business. Edmund C. Lynch was living out of the Twenty-third Street YMCA when he met Merrill. In 1911 Merrill wrote a magazine article titled "Mr. Average Investor." The article focused on the lack of attention the investment customer was typically given. This focus gave way to an investment practice he forged with Lynch in 1914.[2]

10. BENJAMIN GRAHAM (1894-1976)

Known as "The Father of Value Investing," Graham founded many of the fundamental analyses and value-investing prin-

[2] Information gathered from www.merrilllynch.com.

ciples used by many of the sharks of Wall Street. His principles are followed by many fund and portfolio managers
everywhere. He was a professor at Columbia University's
Graduate School of Business from 1924 to 1957, where his
sensible teaching inspired a young student by the name of
Warren Buffett.

Rest in Peace

Everyone is laid to rest somewhere. Often, that somewhere is forgotten and requires a trip off the beaten path. Famous businesspeople as well as other celebrities are buried alongside ordinary people. They may just be at a cemetery near you. Thanks to the good efforts of a wonderful and interesting Web site called www.findagrave.com (the source of the information in this chapter), you can find where almost anyone who's anyone is buried. It's a terrific site, with bountiful information, and is well worth a visit. Where famous businesspeople are buried provides some unexplained fascination. In fact, next time you're at a cocktail party, and the conversation is just blah, try dropping a few of these factoids. You'll become either an amazing hit, or the weird one who talked about gravesites. Here are some notable achievers in the world of business and where they are buried.

1. **EBERHARD ANHEUSER (1805–1880)**
    Grave: Bellefontaine Cemetery, Saint Louis, Missouri
    Founder of the Anheuser-Busch Brewery empire, he first made his fortune in the soap business and then decided to purchase the Bavarian Brewery in 1860. Things changed in

1879 when his daughter married Adolphus Busch, the owner of a brewery supply business, and Anhaeuser-Busch was born.

2.   LEON LEONWOOD "L. L." BEAN (1872–1967)
Grave: Webster Road Cemetery, Freeport, Maine

The mail-order magnate began his business as a supply center for hunters, fishermen, and woodsmen. The company always had a flair of the Maine woods in its offerings and became popular for its traditional and practical clothing and wear. Today, L. L. Bean is virtually a household name, recognized by many throughout the world.

3.   MAX FACTOR (1877–1938)
Grave: Hillside Memorial Park, Culver City, California

The magnate of makeup, Max Factor was born in Poland and came to the United States in 1904. When the fledgling movie industry started to take off, Factor, who popularized the word "makeup," began providing makeup to the stars and in the 1930s developed the formula for Pan-Cake. He built an empire on the world's vanity and desire to look good!

4.   JULIO GALLO (1910–1993)
Grave: Saint Stanislaus Cemetery, Modesto, California

The world-renowned vintner was the co-owner of Ernest and Julio Gallo Winery, in Modesto, California. He died after a jeep accident on his property. His gravestone bears an imprint of grapes and reads "winemaker who loved the land."

5.   BENJAMIN FRANKLIN "B. F." GOODRICH (1841–1888)
Grave: Lake View Cemetery, Jamestown, New York

Born in Ripley, New York, Goodrich was a Union Army surgeon who pioneered the manufacturing of fire hoses and other rubber products before the automobile revolution in the twentieth century. While the company that bears his name is centered in Akron, Ohio—now known as the Rubber Capital of the World—he originally founded the firm in 1869 in upstate New York. He died in a hotel room in Manitou Springs, Colorado, after suffering a severe hemorrhage.

6. HENRY JOHN HEINZ (1844–1916)
Grave: Homewood Cemetery, Pittsburgh, Pennsylvania

His ketchup wasn't introduced until some sixteen years after young Henry Heinz began peddling homegrown vegetables to his Pittsburgh neighbors. Despite ups and downs, the company became a mainstay in the processed foods industry.

7. ORVILLE REDENBACHER (1907–1995)
Grave: Redenbacher's remains were cremated and his ashes scattered at sea

Redenbacher was the man with the bowtie who put flair into popcorn. He studied agronomy at Purdue University and with partner Charles Bowman went on to develop a hybrid popcorn that produced larger kernels. His popcorn became a major player on the shelf for microwave and unpopped popcorn. Redenbacher drowned in a whirlpool after suffering a heart attack on September 19, 1995, near San Diego.

8. HARRY BURNETT REESE (1879–1956)
Grave: Hershey Cemetery, Hershey, Pennsylvania

The man behind Reese's Peanut Butter Cups actually began making his product in the candy town popularized by Milton Hershey—Hershey, Pennsylvania. Even a war shortage of sugar in the United States couldn't stop the peanut butter cups from making it to market. It is one of the best selling candy items in America.

9. JOHN BATTERSON STETSON (1830–1906)
Grave: West Laurel Hill Cemetery, Bala-Cynwyd, Pennsylvania

Born in Orange, New Jersey, Stetson is the father of the ten-gallon Stetson hat. After being diagnosed with tuberculosis, he moved to the West, hoping that the climate would im-

prove his health. In 1885 he returned to the East and established the John B. Stetson Company. After creating a legacy
of Western wear, Stetson died in 1906, leaving an estate of
seven million dollars.

10. CARL A. SWANSON (1874–1949)
Grave: Forest Lawn Cemetery, Omaha, Nebraska

The father of the TV dinner, Carl Swanson still has a stronghold in the frozen foods section of most any supermarket.
Swanson founded the company that actually was built under
the leadership of his son. His idea was to popularize the convenience aspect of food. This concept would later be a major
movement in the packaged foods industry. Incidentally, the
first TV dinner consisted of turkey, cornbread dressing and
gravy, buttered peas, and sweet potatoes.

Businessmen Philanthropists Worth Talking About

S ome people think that nice guys don't finish first, but guys who finish first can still be nice—nice and generous, that is. If you've got it, spend it. If you've got a heart, spend on those in need. Look at some of the greatest philanthropists in history, and you'll see myriad good works created by the generosity of business leaders.

1. ANDREW CARNEGIE (1835–1919)

The industrialist is the quintessential example of how a fortune can be redistributed through charities. Carnegie, who came from humble Scottish roots, built his fortune in steel. His wealth was valued at nearly $350 million at the peak of his career when he sold his steel concern to J. P. Morgan. This equates to a present sum of about $3 billion. Carnegie gave nearly all of it away to various interests ranging from New York's Carnegie Hall, to the Carnegie Institute of Technology (now Carnegie Mellon University), and many other foundations and programs. He was very definitive about philanthropy and wrote essays about its necessity in the *North American Review*.

2. JOHN D. ROCKEFELLER (1839–1937)

Virtue just may run in the family. At least it has for the Rockefellers. From his $3.50 per week bookkeeper job, Rockefeller moved into purveying commodities and eventually moved into the oil business. His fortune grew. As a devout Baptist, he was fervently magnanimous to the less fortunate. He gave away some $540 million, which equates to about $6 billion in today's dollars. His son, John D. Jr., who was a more familiar name and face to contemporary culture, followed in his father's footsteps as a business leader and philanthropist.

3. HENRY FORD (1863–1947)

Ford, who left the family farm at age sixteen to go to Detroit, Michigan, and eventually built one of the nation's biggest automobile manufacturers, had a unique character—sometimes tight and stern with his spending but often generous. He paid workers a whopping five dollars per day in 1914. When he died, he left half his fortune as the Ford Foundation, which gives away hundreds of millions of dollars every year.

4. GEORGE SOROS (1930–   )

An inspiring financier if there ever was one, Soros came from humble Jewish Hungarian roots and rose to become one of the world's wealthiest people. His wealth has led to his being philosophical and reflective about his humble beginnings and rise to fortune. Soros has led efforts that aid and support immigrants and alternatives to stern criminal justice and prison systems. He has also funded some rather unusual efforts, including needle exchange programs, legalized marijuana referendums, and assisted suicide referendums. He has given away nearly one third of his $7 billion of net worth to his philanthropic interests.

5. TED TURNER (1938–   )

Listen to him for a while and you may conclude that he doesn't sound like such a nice guy at all. Although his father

Museum of American Financial History

John D. Rockefeller gave away some $540 million,
which equates to about $6 billion in today's dollars.

committed suicide when Turner was twenty-four years old, the media giant has built a mega-fortune to the magnitude of $2.2 billion. But this wiseguy is truly wise underneath and also quite adamant about giving and philanthropy. Turner is notable for giving away nearly 65 percent of his wealth—an inordinate proportion for any philanthropist. His $1 billion donation to the United Nations was specified to be made in ten equal payments over a ten-year period. It was the largest single philanthropic donation in history.

6.　BILL GATES (1955–　)

It's hard to talk about Bill Gates without mentioning his philanthropy. The Harvard dropout founded Microsoft and created an astounding accumulation of wealth. His wife, Melinda, whom he met at Microsoft, is his partner in his philanthropic efforts. The generous couple formed the famed Bill and Melinda Gates Foundation, which you'll find on placards at many public libraries across the country, as it supports computer rooms and education through public libraries. It's rumored that Gates spends as much effort on the distribution of his $17–$20 billion annual philanthropic disbursements as he does on his everyday software business. He and Melinda have to approve donations above a certain dollar amount. He allows his father and foundation director to decide on smaller gifts and grants.

7.　TOM MONAGHAN (1937–　)

The founder of Domino's Pizza isn't good just at bringing pizza to your door. He has also excelled at bringing help to the needy through his philanthropic efforts with Catholic education and services provided by the church. In addition, he has a peculiar philanthropic effort in preserving the works of notable architect Frank Lloyd Wright. The millionaire, whose net worth is in the neighborhood of $350 million, has given much of it away and has served many charitable organizations with funding.

8. SAM WALTON (1919–1992)

The guy who President George H. W. Bush called the man who "epitomized the American Dream" grew up in Oklahoma during the Great Depression and worked his way up to build one of America's most recognized retail institutions. With a down-home spirit and a net worth of about $94 billion, you'd think that Walton would have donated proportionately more of his wealth than his hoity-toity peers. But surprisingly his remaining trust gives only about 1 percent of the total pie annually. Most of it goes to education.

9. PAUL MELLON (1907–1999)

Not every philanthropist in business history has solely focused on the needy, education, and conservation. Some, like Paul Mellon, have focused on culture and the arts. It's important to note that he did donate generously to education concerns but has also made significant contributions to the art world for the benefit of the public good. Chairman of two foundations set up to dispense the family fortune, Mellon also chaired of the National Gallery of Art and donated millions of dollars of fine British and French art to Yale University.

10. JOHN PIERPONT MORGAN (1837–1913)

This American financier may be best known for his financial artistry in breaking a government bond monopoly and in reorganizing America's railroads at a time when rail transportation was blossoming. He was a major benefactor of the Cathedral of St. John the Divine in New York City, the Metropolitan Museum of Art, the New York Public Library, and several other key hospitals and institutions. Morgan adored art and books. He was a preeminent collector of rare books and manuscripts, many which reside in the Pierpont Morgan Library in New York City.

The Different Drummers

LD. It's the two-letter acronym that stands for "learning disabled." This label may be the biggest misnomer in the free world. "Learning differently" might be more apropos. Those who fall into this category have other strengths and characteristics that mimic the geniuses of the world. Unbeknownst to many, a surprising number of people with learning disabilities also have a very high intelligence quotient. As a result, they develop ways to compensate for their disability and very often see things that others don't. This compensation can lead to some significant accomplishments, and such people are well represented in the community of high achievers throughout the business world. Below is a list of ten people who have struggled with some form of a learning disability but who nevertheless made critical achievements in their lives—and trust me, the list of achievers is much longer than this. They walk to a different drummer, and when that drummer beats in rhythm, the results are remarkable.[1]

[1] Information gathered from www.schwablearning.org.

1. CHARLES SCHWAB (1937–   )

Schwab is the founder and chairman of Charles Schwab Corporation, an investment and financial services firm. In 1975 he blazed new trails in the securities industry with the concept of discount brokerage. You've probably seen his photo in Schwab advertisements. He suffered from dyslexia and credits his disability with allowing him to "think out of the box." He discovered his own disability after learning that his son suffered from the same problem. He advocates strongly for those with learning disabilities and believes the hardest part about the disability is its effect on kids' self-esteem if they do not receive appropriate educational intervention at an early age. In 1989 Schwab and his wife, Helen, founded Schwab Learning, which is a nonprofit organization that aspires to help kids with learning and attention problems to lead satisfying and productive lives in an environment that recognizes, values, and supports the unique attributes of every child.

2. RICHARD BRANSON (1950–   )

Branson is the energetic founder of Virgin Enterprises and suffers from dyslexia. At eight years old, this entrepreneur still couldn't read. Branson himself said of his experiences, "I was soon being beaten once or twice a week for doing poor class work or confusing the date of the Battle of Hastings." His business creation is a conglomerate of companies and businesses, including Virgin Records and Virgin Airlines. He was knighted in 1999 for his business prowess, and in September 2004 he announced plans for a space tourism company, Virgin Galactic.

3. ALBERT EINSTEIN (1874–1955)

Best known for his theory of relativity, Einstein was called lazy and slow by some of his grade school teachers. He was one of the greatest scientists of all time and a nuclear physicist who explained profound scientific principles that indirectly touch our lives each day. His research and findings have inspired further scientific research that helps us understand the physical properties of the world we live in.

4. CRAIG MCCAW (1949–)

The name may not jump out at you, but if you own a cell phone, McCaw may have helped to get it into your hands. The billionaire entrepreneur built a successful cable business and then developed the cellular industry with his company McCaw Cellular, which he sold to AT&T for a handsome profit. In his youth he struggled with dyslexia, but he overcame it with tenacity, graduated from Stanford University, and became a successful entrepreneur.

5. LOUIS PASTEUR (1822–1895)

Pasteur was a notable scientist whose pursuits in chemistry and medicine would greatly change humankind and the health industry. Pasteur suffered from dyslexia and dysgraphia—learning disabilities related to reading and writing, respectively. His legacy is preserved in many theories and practices of science, including "pasteurization," which is derived from his name.

6. TOMMY HILFIGER (1951–)

Notable for his artistic menswear fashions, this award-winning designer described his education as purely struggle. "I performed poorly at school, when I attended, that is, and was perceived as stupid because of my dyslexia. I still have trouble reading." He has built a notable niche label in the world of fashion design.

7. WILBUR WRIGHT (1867–1912)

With his brother, Orville, he invented and built the first successful airplane. Their first flight in Kitty Hawk, North Carolina, gave rise to the modern epoch of aviation as an industry and the most important medium of transportation. Wilbur Wright suffered from dyslexia.

8. **WALT DISNEY (1901–1966)**

Disney began his career as a freelance cartoonist and illustrator and created the character Mickey Mouse. While pushing his daughter on a swing, he often mused about the concept of an entertainment theme park that children and adults could visit and enjoy as a family. Despite suffering from dyslexia, Disney won twenty-nine Oscars, opened Disneyland in 1955, and created the world's largest family entertainment empire.

9. **PAUL ORFALEA (1948–   )**

The founder of Kinko's Copy Centers suffered from severe dyslexia and could barely read by seventh grade. He did go on to college in northern California despite his great struggle with spelling and reading, and rented a garage for $100 per month where he operated a copy shop business for the university community. His business blossomed into the company known as Kinko's, which recently merged with corporate giant FedEx.

10. **JOHN CHAMBERS (1949–   )**

Chambers is the president and chief executive officer of Cisco Systems. Cisco makes some 80 percent of the routers through which information passes on the Internet. Chambers came from Charleston, West Virginia, the son of two doctors. Despite having mild dyslexia, he graduated second in his class from high school. He persevered to overcome his learning disability through hard work and tutoring. Even to this day he dislikes lengthy written memos, preferring to communicate verbally. His presentations are almost thoroughly memorized and dynamically delivered, underscoring the preacherlike flair with which he addresses audiences.

Presidential Business Oddities

Most of our presidents influence the economy and big business regardless of their educational and professional backgrounds. What you may not know is that many of them had some business affiliation before coming to office. Here are a few presidents who fit the category.[1]

1. HARRY S. TRUMAN (1884–1972)

Harry Truman was born in a small town in Missouri in 1884. In his adult life he prospered as a Missouri farmer for twelve years. After returning from World War I, he got married and opened a men's haberdashery in downtown Kansas City, Missouri, which went under in the recession of 1922. This business failure prompted him to consider a full-time career in politics.

2. ANDREW JACKSON (1767–1845)

Jackson was born in the backwoods of the Carolinas in 1767. His education was interspersed at various points in his upbringing. In his late teens he began to school himself in law, and he became a lawyer in Tennessee. However, not all

---

[1] Information gathered from www.whitehouse.gov.

of his avocations were virtuous. He delved into the racetrack business and was a successful gambler. It wasn't until he was a U.S. Army general that he began to recognize a return on his earlier business investments in land speculation.

3. HERBERT HOOVER (1874–1964)

The first American president born west of the Mississippi River, Hoover was born in Iowa in 1874, but came of age in Oregon. He studied at Stanford University as one of its first students in 1891. Hoover graduated as a mining engineer and took on a series of jobs with mining consulting firms, most notably in China. Such exposure allowed him to invest in mining properties. Due to his shrewd speculation, by 1908 Hoover was earning nearly $100,000 per year.

4. GEORGE W. BUSH (1946–)

Bush is said to be the first MBA president. After graduating from Yale University in 1968, he earned his Master of Business Administration from Harvard Business School in 1975. Then it was back to Midland, Texas, to get into the energy business. He collaborated with a group of associates to purchase the Texas Rangers baseball franchise in 1989. Bush was actually a managing general partner of the Texas Rangers until he was elected governor of Texas on November 8, 1994.

5. THOMAS JEFFERSON (1743–1826)

Jefferson was quite an entrepreneur. Though he's well known for his advocacy of liberty and democracy in government, Jefferson was a slave owner who inherited some five thousand acres of land from his father. Jefferson was a lawyer, planter, and surveyor before his terms as president. Although he pursued many business interests along these avocations, he was often in deep debt.

6. GEORGE H. W. BUSH (1924–)

Upon his graduation from Yale University, the senior Bush entered the oil industry of western Texas. He was an oilfield supply salesman for Dresser Industries in Odessa, Texas. The enterprising future president began his own oil drilling company. This firm would merge in 1954 to become the Zapata Offshore Company, which eventually helped him become a millionaire.

7. JIMMY CARTER (1924–)

Jimmy Carter left the peanut fields of Plains, Georgia, to spend seven years as a naval officer. He then returned to Plains to become a peanut farmer and warehouse owner. His father had built a family peanut business and later branched out into commodities brokering, a general store, and other business ventures. Carter's management experience would later be transferred to building and running very notable nonprofit organizations such as the Carter Center and Habitat for Humanity. A *Time* magazine article called him "the best ex-president the U.S. has had since Herbert Hoover."

8. WOODROW WILSON (1856–1924)

Wilson was well educated, having graduated from Princeton University and the University of Virginia Law School. One of his first stints was as a small business owner when he and a friend tried to start a law practice in Atlanta, Georgia, but due to a lack of clients, couldn't pay the rent. He then went to get a doctorate at Johns Hopkins University, entered a career in academia, and eventually rose to the Oval Office.

9. MILLARD FILLMORE (1800–1874)

Fillmore came from the Finger Lakes region of New York, which was backwoods country in those days. Though he worked on his family farm in his early years, at age fifteen he was apprenticed to a cloth dresser. He later studied law and was admitted to the bar in 1823. Fillmore is one of only two presidents (the other being Andrew Jackson) who was actually an indentured servant before his rise to the presidency.

10. ANDREW JOHNSON (1808–1875)

Johnson grew up dirt poor in Raleigh, North Carolina. Similarly to Fillmore, Johnson was apprenticed to a tailor as a boy. He later ran away from home and opened a tailor shop in Greeneville, Tennessee, before entering the world of politics.

Card Sharks

A few years back, during the financially aggressive years of the 1980s when everything corporate was raided, taken over, or just outright exploited, there was a book called *Liar's Poker*. It examined the dog-eat-dog culture of Wall Street and spoke volumes for that morsel of the human character that seems to be present in the genes of the greedy.

Now, this may be an exaggeration, but card games seem to be the perfect method for a polished investor or businessperson to hone his or her judgment and risk taking. Here are some card players who may lay some of the credit for their success on their ability to know when to hold 'em.

1. **BILL GATES (1955–)**

The Microsoft founder is said to have a vast enthusiasm for the game of bridge. His investment guru friend Warren Buffet is also an avid bridge player, and it is said that Gates and Buffet have more than once met for twenty-four-hour killer sessions of contract bridge.

2. **WARREN BUFFET (1930–)**

Buffet boasts a love of the simple things like a good steak dinner and ice cream sodas from Farrell's Ice Cream Parlor and Dairy Queen; he bought a large amount of stock in the latter. His trademark is his no-nonsense, systematic approach to value investing that he learned from his Columbia University Business School professors. He also believes in buying a piece of a business he can understand and comprehend; it must be a business that makes sense to him. He doesn't sound like much of a card shark, but Buffet loves the skill and luck of the draw in a game of bridge, for which he has a passion.

3. MALCOLM FORBES (1919–1990)

The father of Steve Forbes, Malcolm was often seen riding about on his Harley Davidson motorcycles or dabbling with his collection of deftly painted cloisonné eggs, but he had another passion that didn't get as much notice. He played bridge and urged others to play the game to strengthen their minds.

4. HUGH HEFNER (1926–   )

In the early 1950s, Hefner, an aspiring cartoonist, founded the highly successful *Playboy* magazine. Hefner has developed an image as a showman and womanizer. He commonly has been seen in his smoking robe with gorgeous starlings on each arm. Behind this persona is an intellectual competitor who enjoys the game of bridge and likes to test his ability to play.

5. LAURENCE TISCH (1923–2003)

He was the man behind Tisch Hotels and later went on a binge of acquisitions, taking over companies like Lorillard Tobacco, Bulova Watch Company, Loews Corporation, and CBS. The mogul from humble roots in Bensonhurst, Brooklyn, was also an avid bridge player.

6. JACK DREYFUS (1913–   )

This prominent name in the financial landscape is the founder of the Dreyfus Fund Group. Like many of the Wall

Street set, he seems to have the fiery edge of competitive sport found in a card game. Known as "the Lion of Wall Street," Dreyfus qualified for the Masters Bridge Tournament when he was twenty-eight. When he was thirty, he devised a scientific method of playing gin rummy and beat the best players. Dreyfus was reputed to be the best gin rummy player in the United States for many years.

7. JACK WELCH (1935–   )

The dynamo who made GE a fixture of the U.S. Gross National Product, economy, and stock market, Welch is a feisty Irishman from a Boston suburb. He overcame his speech impediment and was frequently competitive in games of hockey and gin rummy, which he played often with his mother.

8. GEORGE SOROS (1930–   )

Soros was a pauper immigrant who learned the ins and outs of stock market investing and rose to be a multibillionaire investment tycoon. When George Soros speaks, people don't just listen, they also watch and hope their money is in the right place. The Hungarian immigrant, who comes from a family that escaped the Nazi holocaust, has had a very lucrative career through his speculative pursuits. It's no wonder that Soros unwinds in the same sport that made him billions—the art of knowing when to hold 'em and when to fold 'em. Soros is an avid poker player.

9. CARL ICAHN (1936–   )

Known over the decades as one of corporate America's most pernicious corporate raiders, Icahn does what any good risk taker does—he plays poker in his spare time. The mark of this self-made billionaire has struck such huge companies as U.S. Steel, Texaco, and TWA. Call it brazen speculation, but Icahn seems to have received his education at the poker table, and it has prepared him well in the art of the ante.

10. **SAM WAKSAL (1949–)**

Well, not all poker players win. Sam Waksal certainly did not. But certainly he would have rather lost at poker, a famous pastime, than with his company, ImClone, which went down as a result of alleged insider trading. Some of that information made its way to none other than domestic goddess Martha Stewart. The whole mess raised much controversy and landed both Stewart and Waksal in jail.

Fore!

G olf just may be the official sport of America's board-
room. If many deals really are struck on the golf course,
one had better watch out when playing a round of golf with
these chief executive officers. *Golf Digest* magazine rates the
golf handicaps of chief executives every two years. Therefore the list is ever changing as superstar golfers come and
go. There are many rumors that as the CEO's golf game
goes, so goes the company. For whatever it's worth, here are
a few hotsy-totsy top executives who have some of the low-
est handicaps in the old-boy network.[1]

1. SCOTT G. MCNEALY, SUN MICROSYSTEMS
Handicap: 3.3

The company is just over twenty years old and is the inventor
of the workstation. Today it leads the way in networked products, servers, workstation computers, and storage products.
It seems McNealy runs the company the way he plays golf,
because he is certainly one of the best.

[1] Handicaps are from *Golf Digest,* March 2000, and www.surferess
.com/ceo.

2. **ROBERT D. WALTER, CARDInAL HEALTH SYSTEMS**
Handicap: 3.6

If golf is good for your health, Robert Walter is living proof that good golf leads the way to good health . . . services. The pharmaceutical distribution and provider services segment is a leading wholesale distributor of pharmaceutical and health care products to drug stores, hospitals, and other health-related distribution arms.

3. **EDWARD A. BLECHSCHMIDT, OLSTEn**
Handicap: 3.9

Edward Blechschmidt can swing a club better than most in Olsten Services, a worldwide staffing firm serving a multitude of labor markets. It's the strategy of the good walk spoiled by a little white ball that he must transfer to his company and its age-old service of placing people in jobs.

4. **WILLIAM DILLARD II, DILLARD'S**
Handicap: 4.0

Golf must be a family tradition, because the rest of William Dillard's business is. Present day Dillard's is the result of a department store founded in 1938 by William Dillard. Over sixty years later, the company operates 337 traditional department stores in 29 states. Don't be surprised if you see golf clothes in the store's clothing line!

5. **RICHARD A. SnELL, FEDERAL-MOGUL**
Handicap: 4.3

They don't drive automobiles on the golf course, but that doesn't stop Richard Snell from having a pretty darn good handicap. Federal-Mogul is a global supplier of automotive components and subsystems, serving the world's original equipment manufacturers and the aftermarket.

6. **PAUL B. FIREMAn, REEBOK InTERnATIOnAL**
Handicap: 5.1

You may have thought that the top corporate golfers would be from sports-oriented companies. Well, as the leader of

Reebok International, Paul Fireman lends some truth to such thinking. With a history dating back to the 1890s, the company now holds the number-two position as a distributor of sports, fitness, and casual footwear, apparel, and equipment. (Somewhere in its line of products you'll find golf shoes.) It's doubtful that these are what makes Paul Fireman pretty hard to beat on the course, but with a 5.1 handicap, Reebok may just lay claim to having an in-house golf expert.

7. JOEL W. JOHNSON, HORMEL FOODS
Handicap: 5.3

When George Hormel started Hormel Foods in 1891, he probably never thought that his company would one day be led by a top-shot golfer. When he's not on the golf course, Joel Johnson leads a company that makes everything from canned chili to packaged bologna. He knows how to slice 'em and drive home a winning effort.

8. L. PHILLIP HUMANN, SUNTRUST BANKS
Handicap: 6.0

Philip Humann puts trust not only in Suntrust but also in his foursome on the links, as he shoots a pretty good round of golf. Many bankers find their way onto the golf course, but not all find their way into the top ten. Humann is the honorary banker golfer who seems to stay out of the rough.

9. CHARLES R. SCHWAB, CHARLES SCHWAB
Handicap: 6.1

It seems that many financiers are top-flight golfers. Charles Schwab, whose smiling face you see on every mutual fund advertisement in major financial magazines is the man—the golfer man, that is. Combine his handicap with Humann's, and you get the financial services sector as the dominant industry group of low-handicapped golfer gurus in corporate America.

10. **EDGAR R. BROOKS, CENTRAL & SOUTH WEST**
Handicap: 6.3

Before his firm merged with American Electric Power in the late 1990s, Brooks's day job was to put power in the pipeline for residences and commercial entities. On the golf course, he puts power in his shots and strokes, to rack up a handicap that puts him in the pack of top CEO golfers.

The Coming of the African American Business

M any African Americans made early progress in starting a business, despite obstacles, and that spirit has carried through to the twenty-first century. Entrepreneurs of African American descent are responsible for starting and developing businesses and institutions that we live with every day. Here are a few who did just that.

1. BOOKER T. WASHINGTON (1856-1915)

On April 5, 1856, Washington was born into slavery on a 207-acre tobacco farm. The realities of life as a slave in the Piedmont region of Virginia, the quest by African Americans for education and equality, and the postwar struggle over political participation all shaped the options and choices of Booker T. Washington. He founded Tuskegee Institute in Alabama in 1881 and later became an important and controversial leader at a time when increasing racism in the United States meant African Americans were subjected to a new era of legalized oppression.

2. ROBERT S. ABBOTT (1868-1940)

Abbott was the founder of the *Chicago Defender*, a Chicago newspaper that exposed issues facing African Americans at the turn of the century. The *Chicago Defender* appeared on May 5, 1905. In 1912 the *Defender* began selling on the newsstands. Abbott sold his paper, obtained advertisements, and collected the news.

3.   HENRY GREEN PARKS JR. (1916–1989)

In 1951 Henry Green Parks Jr., an African American marketer, founded the Parks Sausage Company. Four years later the company launched an ad campaign of "More Parks sausages, Mom, please?" Based in Baltimore, in 1969 Parks Sausage became the first publicly traded black business in America.

4.   WALLY AMOS (1936–   )

As founder of the Famous Amos Chocolate Chip Cookie Company, Amos came to be known as "the face that launched a thousand chips." While working as a talent agent for the prestigious William Morris Agency, Amos used his bite-sized cookies as a sort of edible business card. When friends and clients suggested he sell the promotional cookies, he launched the Famous Amos Cookie Company in 1975 from a Sunset Boulevard storefront in Hollywood. The company would soon become a $10 million a year business.

5.   JOHN HAROLD JOHNSON (1918–   )

Managing editor of his school paper and business manager of his high school yearbook, Johnson went on to the University of Chicago and Northwestern University. He later conceived the idea of a magazine for African Americans and with a $500 loan started *Negro Digest* in 1942. He later launched *Ebony* and other magazines, such as *Jet*, and then expanded the Johnson Publishing Company to include books, radio broadcasting, insurance, and cosmetics manufacturing.

6.   SAMUEL FRAUNCES (1722–1795)

Fraunces was a free black merchant in New York City during the latter part of the eighteenth century. For twenty-three years he owned and operated a tavern on the southern edge of Manhattan. In 1768 the first New York Chamber of Commerce was created in Fraunces Tavern, and the three-story brick mansion was later the site where the Sons of Liberty gathered to mobilize popular sentiment for the coming revolution against the British Crown. The tavern is alive and well today at the corner of Broad and Pearl in New York City and is a major historic site in the area.

7. PAUL CUFFE (1759–1817)

Brought to Massachusetts as a slave at the age of ten, Cuffe became a skilled carpenter after his own industrious efforts enabled him to purchase his personal freedom from slavery by making a payment. With the outbreak of the American Revolution, he and his brother built their own boat and began to run American supplies. This small enterprise grew to become a fleet of merchant vessels and also included a shipyard, making him one of the wealthiest men in America.

8. GEORGE E. JOHNSON (1927–   )

From his humble roots as a sharecropper's son, Johnson worked in a cafeteria, shined shoes, and collected bottles to make ends meet. In 1954 he went to work for the black-owned cosmetics firm Fuller Products. Later, with the help of his wife, he began manufacturing hair-care products and operated the business out of the back of their car. Johnson Products came to be recognized as an innovator in the beauty-care industry, and in 1971 became the first African American–owned business to be listed on the American Stock Exchange.

9. H. C. HAYNES

If form follows function, Haynes seemed to discover that fact. While working as a barber's apprentice, Haynes realized that he needed to be able to resharpen the razor. He used a leather sharpening strap, often located right at the chair, to sharpen the razor. The barber/inventor came up with the invention of the leather "razor strop" in 1899. He went on to sell his innovation and profit from it.

10. **DON CORNELIUS (1936–   )**

In 1967 Cornelius was offered a part-time position as a news announcer on Chicago radio station WVON, one of Chicago's most popular black-oriented stations. Later he would set his sights on TV and TV production, which led to his idea for a black-oriented dance show. Cornelius went on to become the founder and executive producer of *Soul Train*, a weekly dance show. The series first appeared in 1970 in Chicago and would become one of the longest-running TV programs of any genre in the entire history of first-run, nationally syndicated TV programming.

If You Can Make It There, You'll Make It Anywhere

While there have been many secretaries of the treasury, the path getting there has been varied. Some were university professors, military officers, business owners, or managers. As strange as it may sound, it is true: almost all of them had some dealing with New York. The moral of the story? If you want to be secretary of the treasury, it can't hurt to have done a gig in New York state somewhere along the line. Here are ten secretaries of the treasury with some business history in New York.[1]

1. HENRY MORGENTHAU JR. (1891–1967)

Morgenthau served as treasury secretary from January 1, 1934, to July 22, 1945, under President Franklin Delano Roosevelt. Morgenthau had purchased a farm earlier in nearby Dutchess County, New York, where he was a dairy farmer and apple grower. Morgenthau published the *American Agriculturalist* before being appointed to governmental positions where he worked under Roosevelt when the latter was governor.

[1] Information gathered from www.treas.gov.

2. OGDEN L. MILLS (1884–1937)

Mills served as secretary of the treasury from February 13, 1932, to March 4, 1933, under President Herbert Hoover. Mills had been a staunch Republican who until eight years earlier served as treasurer of the Republican County Committee of New York. After losing a congressional race some twenty years earlier, he stuck to his political pursuits and was elected to the New York State Senate in 1914. He didn't give up on his congressional pursuits either. In 1921 he made a successful run for Congress in his New York district and served three terms. These accomplishments were followed by his appointment as secretary of the treasury in 1932.

3. ALEXANDER HAMILTON (1757–1804)

The first secretary of the treasury, Hamilton served from September 11, 1789, to January 31, 1795, under the father of our country, President George Washington. After serving as a member of the Continental Congress, at age twenty-five he opened his own law office in New York City. He served in the New York State Legislature and attended the Philadelphia Convention in 1787, all prior to his treasury post.

4. JOHN A. DIX (1798–1879)

Dix served as secretary of the treasury from January 15, 1861, to March 6, 1861, under President James Buchanan. Dix had some previous ties to New York as a New York state senator and as postmaster for the Empire State.

5. JOHN SHERMAN (1823–1900)

Sherman served as secretary of the treasury from March 10, 1877, to March 3, 1881, under President Rutherford B. Hayes. The eighth of eleven children, Sherman was born in Utica, New York. He was involved in the public policy debate over the redemption of notes for gold and was successful in keeping down any ire of note holders wanting to exchange their notes for the gold that backed it. This led to the New

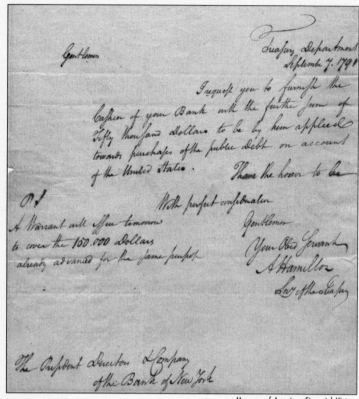

In this letter, Hamilton instructs the Bank of New York to continued making open market purchases of U.S. Treasury bonds.

York Chamber of Commerce requesting that his oil portrait be placed on the chamber walls. Such an honor was bestowed only to Sherman and Alexander Hamilton.

6. C. DOUGLAS DILLON (1909–2003)

Dillon was secretary of the treasury from January 21, 1961, to April 1, 1965. He served under Presidents John F. Kennedy and Lyndon B. Johnson. Earlier, in 1938, he worked as a director of Dillon, Read, and Company, Inc., which his father founded. He was later elected the company's chairman of the board. Dillon had been an investment banker with much international exposure prior to entering government service. At age twenty-two he held a seat on the New York Stock Exchange.

7. **WILLIAM E. SIMON (1927–2000)**

Simon was secretary of the treasury from May 8, 1974, to January 20, 1977. He served under Presidents Richard M. Nixon and Gerald R. Ford. Simon was born in Paterson, New Jersey, just outside of New York City, and was the son of an insurance executive. He worked in investments and had an early stint with Union Securities. Later he worked his way up to vice president of Weeden and Company. He eventually became the senior partner in charge of the government and municipal bond departments at New York–based Salomon Brothers.

8. **DONALD T. REGAN (1918–2003)**

Regan served as secretary of the treasury from January 22, 1981, to February 1, 1985, under President Ronald Reagan. Regan was a notable business leader who had previously served as chairman and chief executive officer of Merrill Lynch and Company, Inc. He rose to this post from earlier jobs at Merrill Lynch's trading department in New York, after which he held other positions in their Philadelphia office and in their administrative division before rising to the chairman's position.

9. **NICHOLAS F. BRADY (1930–)**

Brady was secretary of the treasury from September 15, 1988, to January 17, 1993, under Presidents Ronald Reagan and George H. W. Bush. Brady was born in New York City on April 11, 1930. Like some other secretaries of the treasury, Brady worked for Dillon, Read, and Company, Inc. and eventually became chairman of the board. He was a member of the prestigious board of the Economic Club of New York.

10.   **ROBERT E. RUBIN (1938–)**

Rubin served as secretary of the treasury from January 10, 1995, to July 2, 1999, under President Bill Clinton. Like many before him, Rubin worked the canyons of Wall Street and always seemed to have a New York connection. Before working as an attorney at the firm of Cleary, Gottlieb, Steen, and Hamilton in New York, Rubin had served on the board of directors for several New York–based companies and organizations. He later spent twenty-six years at Goldman Sachs and Company in New York, rising from the rank of associate.

It's a Hard-Knock Life . . .

A t least it was for Li'l Orphan Annie. But the good news for those who were separated from their birth parents is that adoption, and the good graces of the homes that took them in, gives a new outlook for their lives. Adoptees and orphans are all around us, and we often never really know their situation. In the world of business, there have been a number of movers and shakers who were adopted as children. Here are some who were just that.[1]

1. TOM MONAGHAN, DOMINO'S PIZZA (1937–)

When Monaghan was just four years old, his father died on Christmas Eve. Unable to care for her children, his mother gave them up for adoption. Monaghan and his brother spent their childhoods in and out of Catholic orphanages and on work farms in Michigan until they were eventually adopted.

2. BILL CLINTON, 42ND PRESIDENT (1946–)

Did he shape business history? Well, under his reign we witnessed one of the greatest bull runs in a long while. Clinton was known as Billy Blythe until he was adopted at age four

---

[1] Information gathered from *www.ivillage.com*.

by Roger Clinton, his stepfather. He grew up to be an over-
achiever and, well, heck—president of the United States.
Whether it's related to his adoption or not, Clinton has been
described as possessing a need to control situations to avoid
rejection and disapproval. His presidential experience put
that need through the wringer.

3. DAVE THOMAS, WENDY'S (1932–2002)

Adopted at six weeks old, Thomas himself was a major advocate for adoption. He tried to make adoption causes a full-
time agenda by establishing the Dave Thomas Foundation
for Adoption and writing thousands of personal appeals to
organizational leaders in an effort to persuade them to provide adoption assistance in their company benefits plans. He
also lobbied for legislation that would promote the foster-
care system and make adoption affordable.

4. ANDY BERLIN, GOODBY, SILVERSTEIN & PARTNERS (1950–)

Berlin was adopted at an early age. He attended Germantown Academy in Germantown, Pennsylvania, as a child,
where he played football and wrote prize-winning prose and
poetry. He always had a sense of being "different" and even
imagined that his parents were Martians. His background
was the basis for his creative career as an advertising copy-
writer and later entrepreneur. He would eventually create his
existing advertising agency, Goodby, Silverstein & Partners.

5. STEVE JOBS, APPLE COMPUTER COMPANY AND PIXAR (1955–)

He's been called arrogant, egotistical, and true-blue renegade in the ranks of enterprising young turks, but you can't
argue much with his success. Jobs was adopted as an infant
by a machinist in northern California. Through his "Home-
brew Computer Club" beginnings, Jobs evolved the ideas
and technologies into a higher plan. Apple Computer was
born in his garage.

6.   **LARRY ELLISON, ORACLE CORPORATION (1944–   )**

He's in the company of Jobs in being called arrogant, pomp-
ous, egotistical, and, well, successful tech leader. Ellison is
an adoptee, although there aren't too many details about
this. One of the wealthiest people in America, the CEO of the
major database software firm Oracle lives in a $40 million
home, is a notable yachtsman, and owns his own fighter
plane.

7.   **CALVIN GRIFFITH, THE MINNESOTA TWINS (1911–1999)**

Born in Montreal as Calvin Robertson, the former owner of
the Minnesota Twins was involved in baseball all of his life.
In 1960 he moved the Washington Senators to Minnesota to
create the Twins franchise. Griffith began his professional
baseball affiliation as a Washington Senators batboy from
1924 to 1925. It was his uncle Clark Griffith, a Hall of Fame
pitcher on the team, who became his adopted father.

8.   **JOE SENSER, RESTAURANT ENTREPRENEUR (1956–   )**

Raised in the Milton Hershey School for orphans, Senser
played college basketball and football for West Chester University in Pennsylvania. In 1979 he was drafted by the Minnesota Vikings football team and played tight end until 1984.
He now owns several restaurants, including Joe Senser's
Sports Bar and Grill, with locations throughout Minnesota.
He also went on to become the founder of homes for boys
separated from their birth parents.

9.   **PAUL MYNERS, GARTMORE INVESTMENT MANAGEMENT (1948–   )**

Myners grew up in an orphanage in Cornwall, England. He
was later adopted and started his career as a teacher. This
wasn't for long, though, as he soon became involved in business. He rose to chairman of the UK-based Gartmore Investment Management group, where he served until he retired in
2001. He is now chairman of the Guardian Media Group, the

major publisher of newspapers in the UK. He also serves on the boards of several other companies.

10. GEORGE FRANCIS TRAIN, RAILROAD ENTREPRENEUR (1829–1904)

Train wore many hats as an author, orator, businessman, and financial promoter. His parents and siblings died of yellow fever when he was four years old, and his New England grandmother adopted him. In early adulthood he became a successful merchant and shipping magnate and opened his own business in Australia. Of particular note was his introduction of street railways into London and other European cities as well as his assistance in funding the building of the transcontinental railroad. An avid traveler, Train was the inspiration for Jules Verne's *Around the World in Eighty Days.*

It's All in the Family

The family unit is perhaps the cornerstone of American society. When it comes to American enterprise, the family unit has also been a significant building block for the "mom-and-pop" concept of small business. Today we often hear that the big retail chains are crushing smaller businesses, but it's never pointed out that many of the big dogs, too, started out as mom-and-pop shops. Here are ten of the largest family-owned businesses, where members of a single family control ownership of and manage the company, which proves that greatness can come out of even the smallest beginnings.[1]

1. WAL-MART STORES (FOUNDED 1962)

The Walton family founded this discount retail chain based in Bentonville, Arkansas. From their humble beginnings in the early sixties, the firm now anchors many shopping centers all over the world.

2. FORD MOTOR COMPANY (FOUNDED 1903)

At Ford, quality is job one—at least that's what they said in an earlier ad campaign. The Dearborn, Michigan, auto man-

[1] Information gathered from http://familybusinessmagazine.com/top150.html.

ufacturer began when the motorcar was just coming on the scene as a replacement for the horse and buggy. Four generations later, this mainstay in our culture continues to expand and now offers to consumers such models as Mazda, Volvo, Land Rover, Aston Martin, and Jaguar.

3. CARGILL INCORPORATED (FOUNDED 1865)

While it's not exactly a household name like some of the other family-owned businesses, this trader is the world's largest wheeler and dealer of commodities such as grain. The Cargill/MacMillan family founded the company in Minneapolis, Minnesota. Commodities are big business, and Cargill proves it. Think of that when you eat your next bowl of whole-grain cereal.

4. AMERICAN INTERNATIONAL GROUP (FOUNDED 1926)

This may be another name that you may have never heard of, but the Greenberg family in New York, where it remains, founded this insurer in 1926. AIG services range from life insurance and retirement accounts to aircraft leasing. The company racks up over $40 billion by taking risks that others just can't live with, making the company's motto, "we know money," ring true.

5. KOCH INDUSTRIES (FOUNDED 1918)

Oil, gas, and agriculture aren't just the industries behind most of what goes into our homes, gas tanks, and food closets. They're also the ingredients that build Koch Industries. The family-owned firm started in Wichita, Kansas.

6. LOEW'S CORPORATION (FOUNDED 1919)

If you've ever seen a movie in a Loew's Cineplex, just remember that it began as a family-owned gig. The Tisch family of New York founded the firm that owns and operates hotels, theatres, and even tobacco ventures. It has now become a major conglomerate in corporate America.

7. WEYERHAEUSER CORPORATION (FOUNDED 1900)

The next time you see a sheet of plywood, look for a "W" in a triangular logo. If you see it, you've spotted the mark of the Weyerhaeuser family. The business was started in 1900 by Frederick Weyerhaeuser and fifteen partners who capitalized on the lumber needs of a fast-growing nation. Today, the firm makes a multitude of timber-based products, including paper, wood, and pulp, and its home is amid the forests of the western United States in Tacoma, Washington. From its early beginnings, the firm has proved that our society is not yet a paperless society.

8. MARS CORPORATION (FOUNDED 1923)

No, not the planet! Do you remember the Mars bar? Or how about M&M Mars candy? Yes, that's it—such goodies are staple commodities in our pop culture. The Mars Corporation is the business entity that created and produced these candy brands, and they started as a family-owned business. The Mars family began its empire in the early 1920s, and today the McLean, Virginia–based firm still makes a variety of popular candy, as well as rice and pet food.

9. BECHTEL GROUP (FOUNDED 1898)

If you've ever seen a power plant in your neighborhood, Bechtel very well may have had something to do with it. The Bechtel family began its engineering and construction operation in San Francisco, California, at the turn of the twentieth century, and as of 2005 was the world's largest construction company. Among the 22,000 projects the company has participated in are the Hoover dam, the Trans-Arabian pipeline, the Dresden nuclear power plant in Illinois, and the Bay Area Rapid Transit System (BART).

10. GAP (FOUNDED 1969)

The early 1970s was an interesting period for dress, and jeans were very much in during the early part of this decade.

Donald and Doris Fisher opened their first Gap store in the same year that we sent man to the moon, the Grateful Dead played at Woodstock, and the Tet Offensive was launched in Vietnam. Today Gap has some 4,250 stores and helps outfit many with casual clothing.

Leaders Say the Darndest Things

Words of inspiration are fuel for the soul. For the manager, leader, or businessperson they're more like rocket fuel. Here are some quotes on managing that hit the heart and make you want to lead a contingent to victory.[1]

1. HARVEY MACKAY, AUTHOR, MOTIVATIONAL SPEAKER, AND FOUNDER OF MACKAY ENVELOPE COMPANY

"Don't equate activity with efficiency. You are paying your key people to see the big picture. Don't let them get bogged down in a lot of meaningless meetings and paper shuffling. Announce a Friday afternoon off once in a while. Cancel a Monday morning meeting or two. Tell the cast of characters you'd like them to spend the amount of time normally spent preparing for attending the meeting at their desks, simply thinking about an original idea."

[1] Quotes from www.leadershipnow.com/managementquotes.html, www.quotationspage.com, www.brainyquote.com., www.twainquotes.com, and www.marksquotes.com.

2. DAVID OGILVY (1911–1999), ADVERTISING EXECUTIVE AND AGENCY FOUNDER

"Hire people who are better than you are, then leave them to get on with it . . . Look for people who will aim for the remarkable, who will not settle for the routine."

3. RICHARD NIXON (1913–1994), 37TH PRESIDENT OF THE UNITED STATES (UPON HIS RESIGNATION)

"Always give your best, never get discouraged, never be petty; always remember, others may hate you. Those who hate you don't win unless you hate them. And then you destroy yourself."

4. HARRY S. TRUMAN (1884–1972), 33RD PRESIDENT OF THE UNITED STATES

"Men make history and not the other way around. In periods where there is no leadership, society stands still. Progress occurs when courageous, skillful leaders seize the opportunity to change things for the better."

5. ANDREW CARNEGIE (1835–1919), ENTREPRENEUR, INDUSTRIALIST, AND PHILANTHROPIST

"Here is the prime condition of success: Concentrate your energy, thought and capital exclusively upon the business in which you are engaged. Having begun on one line, resolve to fight it out on that line, to lead in it, adopt every improvement, have the best machinery, and know the most about it."

6. GEORGE S. PATTON JR. (1885–1945), AMERICAN GENERAL AND TANK COMMANDER

"The time to take counsel of your fears is before you make an important battle decision. That's the time to listen to every fear you can imagine! When you have collected all the facts and fears and made your decision, turn off all your fears and go ahead!"

7. MARK TWAIN (SAMUEL L. CLEMENS) (1835–1910), AUTHOR AND HUMORIST

"Let your sympathies and your compassion be always with the underdog in the fight—this is magnanimity; but bet on the other one—this is business."

8. SAMUEL J. TILDEN (1814–1886), 1876 DEMOCRATIC CANDIDATE FOR PRESIDENT

"It is said that it is far more difficult to hold and maintain leadership (liberty) than it is to attain it. Success is a ruthless competitor, for it flatters and nourishes our weaknesses and lulls us into complacency. We bask in the sunshine of accomplishment and lose the spirit of humility, which helps us visualize all the factors which have contributed to our success. We are apt to forget that we are only one of a team, that in unity there is strength and that we are strong only as long as each unit in our organization functions with precision."

9. RUPERT MURDOCH (1931–   ), MEDIA MOGUL AND BILLIONAIRE

"In motivating people, you've got to engage their minds and their hearts. It is good business to have an employee feel part of the entire effort; . . . I motivate people, I hope, by example—and perhaps by excitement, by having provocative ideas to make others feel involved."

10. THOMAS JEFFERSON (1743–1826), STATESMAN, INDUSTRIALIST, AND 3RD PRESIDENT OF THE UNITED STATES

"It is of great importance to set a resolution, not to be shaken, never to tell an untruth. There is no vice so mean, so pitiful, so contemptible; and he who permits himself to tell a lie once, finds it much easier to do it a second and third time, till at length it becomes habitual; he tells lies without attending to it, and truths without the world's believing him. This falsehood of the tongue leads to that of the heart, and in time depraves all its good dispositions."

Built to Last

Cornelius Vanderbilt Jr. said, "Until the age of twelve I sincerely believed that everybody had a house on Fifth Avenue, a villa in Newport and a steam-driven, ocean-going yacht." Well, of course this is not the case for all those in business, but it is interesting to explore where the titans of enterprise hang their hats after a hard day at the office. For some, home is a city townhouse. For others, it's a sprawling country estate. Many of these places are still in existence, and all are downright fascinating to hear about.

1. GEORGE WASHINGTON VANDERBILT'S BILTMORE ESTATE (ASHEVILLE, NORTH CAROLINA)

It is as breathtaking and heart-stopping as a home can be. It will take you days to digest it all. Located in the Blue Ridge Mountains, Biltmore Estate is a sprawling array of more than 250 rooms, faithfully preserved and filled with thousands of original furnishings. One of the eight children of William Henry and his wife, Maria Louisa (1821–1896), George Washington Vanderbilt was born in 1862 and was an heir to the Cornelius Vanderbilt fortune. It was while traveling in the mountains of North Carolina that Vanderbilt first glimpsed the site for his future country home. Advertising itself as "America's Largest Home," the Biltmore is a showcase of the finest artisans of its time and is still beautifully preserved today.

2. MARSHALL FIELD'S CAUMSETT (LLOYD HARBOR, NEW YORK)

Caumsett resembled many estates of its day on Long Island's Gold Coast in that it was a self-contained community complete with dairy farm, stables, boating docks, its own power sources, and myriad internal roadways. Marshall Field III, the Chicago department store heir, built the Georgian Revival home on the estate in 1925 and called the land Caumsett, the Matenecock Indian word for "place by a sharp rock." It is now the setting for a state park.

3. WALTER CHRYSLER'S ESTATE (KINGS POINT, NEW YORK)

The auto magnate reportedly bought this estate in 1924 from storeowner Henri Bendel. The thirty-five-room Beaux Arts French Renaissance-style mansion now houses the U.S. Merchant Marine Academy. Chrysler's neighbor was George M. Cohan, and the village of Kings Point was the real live backdrop for F. Scott Fitzgerald's novel *The Great Gatsby*, in which Kings Point was portrayed as West Egg, or so the rumor goes.

4. STEEL MAGNATE HENRY C. FRICK'S PORTFOLIO OF HOMES (PITTSBURGH, SUBURBAN BOSTON, MANHATTAN, AND ROSLYN, NEW YORK)

Henry Clay Frick was partner to Andrew Carnegie's steel empire, but Frick had a falling out with him. He nestled his estate right on Long Island's Gold Coast and kept up with the Joneses of the early part of this century. Frick was a world-famous art collector and never was without a roof over his head, and a stately roof at that. His palaces were characteristic of the gilded age, with priceless works of art and the finest in gardens and grounds. He made his money with Carnegie Steel in Pittsburgh and from 1882 to 1905 lived in a Victorian mansion called Clayton, which in 1990 was opened to the public as the Frick Art and Historical Center. His summer retreat, north of Boston, was a neoclassical, all-brick mansion. Visitors to Manhattan can't miss his eighteenth-century-style mansion at 1 East Seventieth Street, now the home of the internationally known Frick Collection Museum. His fourth house, a Georgian Revival masterpiece in Roslyn, New York, now serves as the Nassau County Museum of Fine Arts.

5. BILL GATES'S HUMBLE ABODE (MEDINA, WASHINGTON)

Well, it can hardly be called humble. The 66,000 square foot elaborate complex on five acres of land is out of the price range of the rich and famous of yesteryear as well as that of modern-day tycoons. Much of the house is built into a hill, and Gates pays about a million dollars a year in taxes on the home. It's also a showcase for technology and gadgets in his tech-savvy theatre. It has a cornucopia of high-flying features, including a fish hatchery, an indoor-outdoor pool, two boat docks, and forty-two lineal feet of clothes-hanging space for his wife, Melinda.

6. ORACLE CEO LARRY ELLISON'S FORT ELLISON (WOODSIDE, CALIFORNIA)

Woodside, California, is home to one of Silicon Valley's most notorious and egocentric business leaders. To Ellison's chagrin, the house, with 7,800 square feet in its main residence, is a bit smaller than Bill Gates's. It is a twenty-three-acre Japanese-style imperial villa valued somewhere around $100 million dollars and incurs more than $400,000 in annual property taxes.

7. WILLIAM RANDOLPH HEARST'S HEARST CASTLE (SAN SIMEON, CALIFORNIA)

William Randolph Hearst built a communications empire. His influence on society was felt through newspapers, books, magazines, and motion pictures. In the 1920s Hearst built a castle on a 240,000-acre ranch in the hills of Southern California that became known as Hearst Castle. Now a state historic site and popular tourist destination, each year over 700,000 visitors take shuttle buses up a long and winding road to arrive at the palatial estate. The castle includes 165 bedrooms, 41 bathrooms, and millions of dollars in paintings, antiques, and statuary.

8. FRANK W. WOOLWORTH'S WINFIELD HALL (GLEN COVE, LONG ISLAND, NEW YORK)

F. W. Woolworth built his chain of stores on the premise that the common workingman needed to shop for sundries also, and his chain provided for that. Woolworth's home, Winfield Hall, was built in 1916. However, Woolworth died two years after its construction. Woolworth's mansion is composed of fifty-six rooms in a Beaux Arts design. Like the many estates of its day, it was adorned with lush complementary gardens and statuary. Woolworth's marble staircase is estimated to have cost two million dollars! It is now a conference center and leased to Pall Corporation based in nearby East Hills, New York.

9. HARRY F. GUGGENHEIM'S FALAISE ESTATE (SANDS POINT, NEW YORK)

Guggenheim's Normandy-style summer home was built in 1923, farther along the road to "West Egg," which is how F. Scott Fitzgerald characterized the area because of the harbor that looked like an egg on a local map. Guggenheim's estate was built as a cluster of structures to look like castles and fortresses and reflected the art and architecture of Medieval and Renaissance Europe. Jewish immigrants, his family earned their fortune in metals mining and smelting, with a sizeable stake in copper extraction. Guggenheim was an aviator, who, like many of the estate owners of the area, helped finance the first transatlantic flight by Charles Lindbergh, a frequent visitor to Falaise. The 216-acre estate is now home to Sands Point Reserve.

10. JOHN PIERPONT MORGAN JR.'S MANHATTAN BROWNSTONE (NEW YORK CITY)

This lavish city brownstone was built in 1853 for financier Isaac N. Phelps and was purchased and remodeled by J. P. Morgan Sr. in 1895. The Manhattan mansion was just one of seven residences owned by J. P. Morgan Jr., who became heir to his father's investment banking fortune. Morgan disliked publicity and was a philanthropist, later endowing the Pierpont Morgan Library in New York City as a research institute in memory of his father. Mr. Morgan's library, as it was known in his lifetime, was built between 1902 and 1906 adjacent to his New York residence at Madison Avenue and 36th Street. On February 26, 2002, the Landmarks Preservation Commission designated the J. P. Morgan Jr. House as a New York City landmark.

The School of
Hard Knocks

E ducation. It's what your parents beat into your head to the point that you beat it into the heads of your kids. But does it make a difference? Well, of course it does. But for many high achievers in the corporate world, a college degree hasn't been a common denominator. Some of the most notable names in business did not complete college. Here are few who did not.

1. BILL GATES (1955–), FOUNDER OF MICROSOFT CORPORATION

He went off to Harvard University to become a high-flying attorney like his father. But when his interest and intellect turned toward computers, he dropped out of Harvard and went on to form his computer software company.

2. STEVEN JOBS (1955–), FOUNDER OF APPLE COMPUTER

Jobs dropped out of Reed College in Portland, Oregon, after one semester. The bright and audacious entrepreneur had a sixth sense for what sort of technology he wanted to see and use, so he launched the Apple computing empire. The kid without a college degree became a household name and a star of the information technology hall of fame.

3. MICHAEL DELL (1965–   ), FOUNDER OF DELL COMPUTER

After one year at the University of Texas in Austin, Dell dropped out when his part-time computer business took off. Today, Michael Dell is a colorful and dynamic speaker. He begins many of his public speaking engagements with mention of the company he started in his garage based on the concept of "build-to-order" technology. No degree, no problem for Michael Dell. But Dell has created big problems for other manufacturers in the PC market who now fight for market share in the arena of personal computers.

4. DAVE THOMAS (1932–2002), FOUNDER OF WENDY'S INTERNATIONAL

He dropped out of school in Fort Wayne, Indiana, in the tenth grade and went to work full-time at a local restaurant. The ambitious Thomas's lack of education never seemed to impede his ability to build a major fast-food corporation, which now has over 4,400 locations in over 34 countries and territories.

5. TED WAITT (1963–   ), GATEWAY COMPUTERS

You've seen the boxes that look like cowhide with a computer inside. By now everyone knows Gateway. Its founder, Ted Waitt, left the University of Iowa in his sophomore year. What he didn't leave was his Iowa agricultural influence, which he turned into a unique image for his own computer company.

6. THOMAS EDISON (1847–1931), INVENTOR

Edison spent three months in school, and then was home-schooled by his mother. At the age of twelve he began his entrepreneurial ventures selling fruit, candy, and newsletters to railroad commuters. He suffered from deafness and later worked his way into a telegraph position with Western Union

Telegraph. The kid with no education is now part of every American child's education.

7. HENRY J. KAISER (1882–1967), INDUSTRIALIST AND ENTREPRENEUR

After leaving school when he was thirteen years old, Henry Kaiser became a photographer's apprentice and bought the business at age twenty. After some career stints in construction and shipbuilding, he became heavily involved in labor relations. In 1942 Kaiser founded the first health maintenance organization, now known as Kaiser Permanente, which grew to become one of the largest HMOs in America. Education or not, he made his mark.

8. TED TURNER (1938–), FOUNDER OF CNN

Turner, always known for his "shoot from the hip" and daredevil demeanor, was expelled from Brown University after he allowed a female guest into his dorm room against regulations. His expulsion didn't stop him though. He later inherited his father's Atlanta-based television station after his father tragically committed suicide. Turner went on to build the station into the CNN media empire that we know today.

9. CHARLES WILLIAM POST (1854–1914), FOUNDER OF THE POST CEREALS TRADEMARK AND BRAND

Post attended Illinois Industrial College (now the University of Illinois) but soon dropped out, believing that school was a waste of time. He manufactured agricultural machines and worked on various inventions. After undergoing medical treatment in Battle Creek, Michigan, Post developed Postum Food Coffee and launched one of the first massive advertising campaigns for a food product. He later introduced Post Grape Nuts and Post Toasties, which illustrate his health-conscious approach to diet. Sadly, Post sporadically suffered from depression and fell victim to suicide after recovering from appendicitis.

10. WALT DISNEY (1901–1966), FOUNDER OF THE DISNEY ENTERTAINMENT CONGLOMERATE

Raised on a Missouri farm, Disney took art lessons through correspondence courses and at a local museum. He was known to have had a learning disability. He later was an apprentice advertising animator after serving in the Red Cross during World War I. Armed with no formal college education but much art instruction and experience as an illustrator, he set out for Hollywood to make animated films with his older brother, Roy, in 1923. Education or not, the Disney name grew, stuck, and is known throughout the world today.

Pool Sharks

Billiards is what it's called if you're serious. Whether it's called pool or billiards, it's one of the most popular pastimes in America. But, interestingly enough, the game has been popular not just among the punks of the Brooklyn Bowery or central to Jim Croce's "Bad, Bad, Leroy Brown," who was the "baddest man in the whole damn town" on the southside of Chicago. No, billiards has been the favorite pastime of many a reputable business leader in the history of American business. Here are some who really played the game.[1]

1. ANDREW CARNEGIE (1835–1919)

The steel magnate and Scottish immigrant who became one of the world's most notable philanthropists wasn't all business. He liked to unwind, unload, and get into it with a game of pool. How'd you like to challenge Andrew Carnegie to a game of billiards?

2. JOHN D. ROCKEFELLER (1839–1937)

The fact that he was a millionaire had no bearing on what games he played. He played the same game as cowboys in a Wild West saloon: billiards.

[1] Information gathered from www.brunswickbilliards.com.

3. WILLIAM VANDERBILT (1821–1885)

It must be something about some of the most notable names in business history, but William Vanderbilt was in the company of many a great person who succeeded in business and also had a great affection for billiards.

4. HENRY FORD (1863–1947)

The grandiose founder of the empire that would become a sizeable portion of our nation's GNP was something of a betting man—"betting" in that he liked to challenge folks to a round of billiards. Ford once said, "Money is like an arm or a leg . . . use it or lose it." Well, he didn't want to lose his arms or legs, so he played billiards. He didn't want to lose his money, so he used it.

5. J. P. MORGAN (1837–1913)

The renowned financier drank the same brew as his cohorts in that he, too, played billiards. He, too, was a tremendous benefactor. Now doesn't that sound familiar? Is there something about the game of billiards that just attracts people like Morgan and his peers? Go figure.

6. WILLIAM RANDOLPH HEARST (1863–1951)

The newspaperman who built a publishing empire and entertained guests at his huge, elegant, grandiose castle at San Simeon, California, was a mainstay in the honor roll of famous Americans in business as well. Had you been a guest to the famous Hearst Castle, you could have swam in his elegant indoor swimming pools or perhaps seen a movie in his private screening room. And while you were there, you just might have been able to challenge the master to a game of billiards.

7. TEDDY ROOSEVELT (1858–1919)

The Trust Buster, Rough Rider colonel, and rugged individualist just never sat still. He was a man of sport and was often busy riding his horse through Washington, D.C.'s Rock Creek Park, hiking a trail in the Adirondacks, or playing ten-

nis with members of his cabinet. Big businessmen of the industrial revolution didn't like him, because he was set to
break up the trusts and monopolistic control of big businesses such as railroads and other industrial concerns. Roosevelt was athletic and used his love of sport and
competition to overcome his problems of poor vision,
asthma, and early childhood ailments. Along with his delight
of hunting, tennis, and cribbage, he was an avid billiards
player.

8. MARK TWAIN (SAMUEL CLEMENS) (1835–1910)

Was he a businessman? You betcha. A failed one. Twain's
wit and wisdom is legendary to anyone with an appreciation
for American literature and humor. He lost almost all the fortune he had gained through his writings when he made a
fledgling investment into a typesetting machine. Nevertheless, Twain bounced back from financial failure and managed to lecture and write his way out of the loss. From his
earliest stints out West as a journalist, Twain discovered the
character and wily ways of the American spirit around the
billiards table. The tables weren't always in the seclusion of
his home, but right where the real people were: the saloon.

9. ABRAHAM LINCOLN (1809–1865)

Honest Abe, who would persuade his law clients to negotiate
a settlement or admit their guilt if they were in fact guilty, led
a stressful life. He suffered the death of a son, depression,
and a presidency with challenges that are forever part of
America's history. So how did he deal with it? Well, there
may be a variety of outlets that Lincoln had, but one of them
was picking up his cue, racking up the balls, and shooting a
game of billiards.

10. BUFFALO BILL CODY (1846–1917), TEXAS JACK UHUMBRO (DATES UNKNOWN), AND WILD BILL HICKOCK (1837–1876)

These three performers were out and about in the 1890s,
touring with their "Wild West" show. The Brunswick Corpo-

ration (a notable manufacturer of billiards tables) tells the story that the three were drinking in a tavern in Boston when a group of longshoremen challenged the outsiders from the West. The cowboys beat the beans out of the Bostonites. Buffalo Bill later stocked his hotel in Cheyenne, Wyoming, with Brunswick billiards tables, as he had a winning spirit and insisted on nothing but the best.

Be Prepared

"Be Prepared" is the motto of the Boy Scouts of America. The youth organization for boys has been around for nearly one hundred years and has instilled the values of teamwork, loyalty, reverence, and great fun in the outdoors. The activity has kept boys out of trouble for most of their young years, and you'll still find them around the globe today, scaling rock walls and cliffs, camping, hiking, canoeing, learning First Aid, and selling popcorn. Scouting works on a rank achievement system, whereby rank is achieved by completing a specified list of goals. The highest and most honorable rank in scouting is that of Eagle Scout. Many high achievers in all walks of life began their adult lives with this achievement. Here are some notable business leaders who have achieved the level of Eagle Scout and one—a very important one—who achieved Life Scout.[1]

1. BARBER B. CONABLE (1922–2003), PRESIDENT, WORLD BANK

Conable was a distinguished professor at the University of Rochester (New York). After graduating from Cornell Univer-

[1] Information gathered from www.scouting.org.

sity, he served in the U.S. Marines in both World War II and the Korean War. Conable also served twenty years as a U.S. congressman from New York before retiring in 1985. From 1977 until his retirement, he was the ranking Republican member of the House Ways and Means Committee. He became president of the World Bank in July 1986, and served until July 1991.

2. J. WILLARD MARRIOTT JR. (1932–   ), PRESIDENT, MARRIOTT INTERNATIONAL, INC.

Succeeding his father, who founded the chain, the younger Marriott led Marriott International, Inc. in growing to over 2,400 hotels in 65 countries and all 50 states. Its sales are in the neighborhood of $20 billion. Marriott served aboard an aircraft carrier in the U.S. Navy as a supply officer and graduated from the University of Utah.

3. JOHN W. CREIGHTON JR., RETIRED PRESIDENT AND CEO OF WEYERHAEUSER COMPANY AND CEO OF UNITED AIRLINES

This U.S. Army veteran is a graduate of Ohio State University and received his MBA from the University of Miami (Florida). Creighton spent many years in the pulp and paper industry before assuming his present leadership position as chief executive officer of United Airlines.

4. H. ROSS PEROT (1930–   ), SELF-MADE BILLIONAIRE AND FORMER PRESIDENTIAL CANDIDATE

This U.S. Naval Academy graduate who founded Electronic Data Systems in Dallas also made major inroads into U.S. government. The most famous of these was his 1992 run for the presidency on an independent ticket where he went up against Bill Clinton and George Bush Sr. and received 18.9 percent of the popular vote. After later forming the Reform Party, he ran for president again in 1996, this time receiving only 9 percent of the popular vote. Before entering the U.S. Naval Academy, Perot achieved the rank of Eagle Scout.

Many years later he was given the honor of Distinguished Eagle Scout.[2]

5. **SAM SKINNER, FORMER U.S. TRANSPORTATION SECRETARY AND PRESIDENT OF COMMONWEALTH EDISON**

In 1989 President George H. W. Bush appointed Skinner to the post of secretary of transportation, where he served for three years. Later, during the first Gulf War he became Bush's chief of staff. Skinner, a Chicago native, attended the University of Illinois and DePaul University Law School and rose to be a U.S. District Attorney in his home state of Illinois. In 2004 he joined the Chicago office of international law firm Greenberg Traurig LLP.

6. **SAM WALTON (1918–1992), FOUNDER, WAL-MART CORPORATION**

A graduate of the University of Missouri and former employee of J. C. Penney, Walton served in the U.S. Army Intelligence Corps and reached the rank of captain. He is most famous for his humble upbringing and "regular guy" management traits in building the retail giant Wal-Mart. Walton drove about in his pickup truck and built Wal-Mart into a superstore with low prices and great variety. He held the position as "the richest man in America" on several occasions before his death from bone cancer in 1992, less than a month after receiving the Presidential Medal of Freedom from President George H. W. Bush. When he was in eighth grade, Walton became the state of Missouri's youngest Eagle Scout.

[2] The Distinguished Eagle Scout Award was established in 1969 to acknowledge Eagle Scouts who have distinguished themselves in business, professions, and service to their country. Only Eagle Scouts who earned the Eagle Scout rank a minimum of twenty-five years previously are eligible for nomination. The award is given by the National Eagle Scout Service upon the recommendation of a committee of Distinguished Eagle Scouts.

7. PERCY SUTTON (1920–   ), ATTORNEY, AND CHAIRMAN OF THE BOARD OF INNER CITY BROADCASTING CORPORATION

Sutton attended three historically black universities without earning a degree—Prairie View Agricultural and Mechanical College, Tuskegee Institute, and Hampton Institute—and then went on to serve as an airman in the U.S. Army. He earned his law degree from Brooklyn College Law School in 1950. Sutton served as a borough president of Manhattan, New York, in the late 1960s and later cofounded the Inner City Broadcasting Company. In 1977 he ran for mayor of the city, but lost to Ed Koch.

8. WILLIAM J. BENNETT (1943–   ), FORMER SECRETARY OF EDUCATION

Raised in Brooklyn in an Irish Catholic background, Bennett was educated in New York and held very strong views on education and the role it plays in serving our youth. He graduated from Williams College, received his PhD from the University of Texas, and got his law degree from Harvard Law School. In 1985 President Ronald Reagan appointed him to the post of secretary of education, where he served until 1988. In 1989 he was appointed as director of the Office of National Drug Control Policy by President George H. W. Bush. Despite being an Eagle Scout and writing the bestselling *Book of Virtues*, in 2003 Bennett admitted having a gambling problem to which he lost millions of dollars. He has since promised to reform his gambling habit.

9. DONALD RUMSFELD (1932–   ), SECRETARY OF DEFENSE

Donald H. Rumsfeld graduated from Princeton University and served as a pilot in the U.S. Navy. He was sworn in as the twenty-first secretary of defense on January 20, 2001. Before assuming his present post, Rumsfeld had also served as the thirteenth secretary of defense, White House Chief of Staff, U.S. Ambassador to NATO, U.S. congressman, and

chief executive officer of two Fortune 500 companies—
General Instrument Corporation and Gilead Sciences, Inc., a
pharmaceutical company. He, too, is a Distinguished Eagle
Scout as well as a recipient of the Presidential Medal of Freedom, which he was honored with in 1977.[3]

10. BILL GATES (1955–   ), FOUNDER OF MICROSOFT CORPORATION

It's difficult to live in this world without knowing who Bill
Gates is. The Harvard dropout founded the Microsoft Corporation in 1975 and has built the company to a preeminent
status in the software industry. His philanthropic activity is
among the highest in history, and when Bill Gates speaks
about technology, everyone seems to listen. He is one scout
who did not quite make the rank of Eagle, but achieved the
next highest rank of Life Scout.

[3] Information gathered from www.defenselink.mil/bios/secdef_
bio.html.

Major Figures before the Great Crash

The stock market crash of October 1929 was a major milestone in the history of the twentieth century, wiping out 40 percent of the paper values of common stocks. Many respectable and intelligent speculators lost their life savings. Four years after the financial fiasco, market value was a mere one-fifth of what it had been. The result was economically grim, with businesses shutting down and banks closing their doors. Overall agricultural production was down, and farm income was halved. A quarter of the workforce was still unemployed three years after the crash.

If you were a fly on the wall of America during the twenty years or so leading up to the crash, who were the voices and the figures that would have shaped your thinking? Here are the names of ten newsworthy people who prefigured the Great Stock Market Crash.

1. J. P. MORGAN JR. (1867–1943)

Morgan took over J. P. Morgan and Company, one of the most prestigious private banking firms in the world. Although Morgan and other financiers bought up stock on "Black Thursday" in an attempt to quash panic and keep the

The headline from the *New York Daily Investment News*,
only four days before the stock market crashed in 1929, read
"Stock Market Crisis Over." Oops!

market afloat, many believed that these same people had some control over the conditions that ultimately led to the crash. The Senate Committee on Banking and Currency later disclosed that J. P. Morgan and Company employed "preferred lists," which enabled influential persons to buy securities at less than the market price.

2. WARREN G. HARDING (1865–1923)

Under his reign as president, the tariff acts of 1922 brought tariff barriers to new heights, with tariffs on some products of up to 400 percent, thus guaranteeing prosperity to U.S. manufacturers. Such monopoly in the domestic market situated all the eggs of American enterprise in the baskets of a few. This risky structure came tumbling down with the market fall.

3. HENRY CANTWELL WALLACE (1866–1924)

Before Wallace became secretary of agriculture in 1921, the American farm experienced a time of great prosperity as farm prices rose to keep up with wartime demand. Such prosperity ignited investment by farmers in capital goods that had been cost prohibitive earlier. By the end of 1920, wartime demand had waned and so did demand for core crops such as wheat and corn. American agriculture was in decline. Because of import tariffs, farmers couldn't sell to foreign markets where the United States was not buying an equivalent amount of goods. During Cantwell's reign as secretary, the landscape of the Great Plains and farm fields was one that would prepare the way for further collapse in 1929.

4. CALVIN COOLIDGE (1872–1933)

"The chief business of the American people is business," declared Calvin Coolidge. Coolidge was a New England Yankee if there ever was one. He was a Vermont-born vice president and later became president in 1923 after the death of Harding. Because Coolidge made few changes in the country's economic plans when he assumed the presidency, many scholars and historians blame the two men for the stock market crash of 1929 as well as the Great Depression.

5. GEORGE W. GOETHALS (1858–1928)

New Yorkers may recognize the name as a bridge connecting New Jersey to New York's Staten Island. But Goethals may also take much credit for the building of the Panama Canal. Completed in 1913, the canal was the great path between the waterways that now opened one world to another and expedited commerce by ship. Goethals was the governor of the Panama Canal Zone by late 1916. The canal also paved the way for exuberant commerce and trading among nations that had been separated by long voyages prior to its construction. Goethals and his creation were part of the backdrop leading up to the great crash of 1929.

6. ANDREW MELLON (1855–1937)

Mellon was a treasury secretary who had an adamant view on income taxes. Mellon believed that a high rate of taxation on people prevented them from investing in new industrial enterprise. Congress favored his position and, about eight years before the great crash, passed a series of laws that reduced wartime taxes on income, excess profit taxes, and corporation taxes. While he served as treasury secretary, America experienced an unprecedented period of financial prosperity.

7. JOHN JAKOB RASKOB (1879–1950)

Raskob best characterizes the thinking of the day. He had been a financial manager for the DuPont Corporation and later General Motors Corporation before the Great Depression. He was Governor Al Smith's campaign manager when he ran for president in 1928. In an article titled "Everybody Ought to be Rich," Raskob declared, "Prosperity is in the nature of an endless chain, and we can break it only by refusing to see what it is." Raskob was responsible for obtaining financing for the building of the Empire State Building.

8. F. SCOTT FITZGERALD (1896–1940)

Fitzgerald is a classic novelist of the Roaring Twenties and was part of a small group of writers who were part of what many called the "Lost Generation." This group was in shock over the carnage of World War I and dismayed with the returning materialism and spiritual emptiness of life in the post-World War I United States. With no idea of what was in store for the country's financial future, Fitzgerald published *The Great Gatsby* in 1925, four years before the stock market crash. Viewed by many as the Great American Novel, the book portrays Nick Carraway and Jay Gatsby, neighbors in the affluent community of West Egg, a community full of lavish lawn parties, covetous love affairs, and a subtle but definite pursuit of greed, wealth, and power that ultimately brings failure.

9. JULIUS H. BARNES

Barnes had been an ardent businessman, rising out of Duluth, Minnesota, not too far from the roots of F. Scott Fitzgerald. He was a major business leader in the wheat and grain industry. His entrance into politics in 1922 as president of the U.S. Chamber of Commerce demonstrated his poise as an avid lobbyist for the free enterprise system. He became a close personal friend of Herbert Hoover and worked undercover for him. Barnes was in no way exempt from market forces. He lost two million dollars in the stock market crash of 1929 but was nevertheless featured on the cover of *Time* magazine in May 1930.

10. HERBERT HOOVER (1874–1964)

Hoover became president only eight months before the market crash. He tried to bring an impoverished nation back to prosperity with little avail. Republican politics and underlying flaws in economic policy were to blame, believed Franklin Delano Roosevelt, the Democrat who was governor of New York at the time. Hoover's Smoot-Hawley Act of 1930 created tariff rates so high that economists were sure recovery would be forever dampened if he did not veto it. Although Hoover believed that the aftershock of a world depression, brought on by an earlier world war, had swirled the local economy into its broken state, he was optimistic that the economy had the fundamental elements to recover.

Better Left Unsaid!

While forecasts, predictions, and promises always make the news of the day, seldom does anyone check on the true validity of the statements. Dig deep and you'll find some words that would better be left unsaid. Here are ten cases of such verbal missteps.[1]

1. IRVING FISHER (1867–1947), PROFESSOR OF ECONOMICS, YALE UNIVERSITY

If you keep your ear to the ground of stock and Wall Street analysts, you will indeed hear this expression in one way or another. At every bout of stock market euphoria, you find someone who claims that stocks just aren't climbing any higher. If history repeats itself, the statement will be incorrect, and indeed it was when shortly before the stock market crash of 1929 Irving Fisher made the following statement: "Stock prices have reached what looks like a permanently high plateau."

[1] Quotes from www.heartquotes.com and *The Book of Truly Stupid Business Quotes*, by Jeff Parietti (New York: HarperPerennial Library, 1997).

2. KEN OLSON, PRESIDENT, CHAIRMAN AND FOUNDER OF DIGITAL EQUIPMENT CORPORATION

In 1977 Olson said: "There is no reason anyone would want a computer in their home." Boy, oh, boy, was *he* ever wrong. Ken Olson, wherever you are—what were you thinking? Today, many of us can't imagine life without computers.

3. WARREN BUFFETT (1930–)

Buffet always believed in buying what you know and could understand. One of his buys was Gillette, which he believed had the "franchise" quality of being able to be in the homes of all the men and women who shave their faces or legs each day. Buffett showed his exuberance for this fact when he said: "I go to bed happy at night knowing that hair is growing on the faces of billions of males and on women's legs around the world while I sleep. It's more fun than counting sheep."

4. MARCI KLEIN (1967–), DAUGHTER OF CALVIN KLEIN

Although it was Brooke Shields whose sexy stardom made Calvin Klein underwear a hot-to-trot television advertisement, Calvin Klein's own daughter wasn't far behind the curve of risqué statements when she said: "My only complaint about having a father in fashion is that every time I'm about to go to bed with a guy, I have to look at my dad's name all over his underwear."

5. DEPARTMENT OF SOCIAL SERVICES, GREENVILLE, SOUTH CAROLINA

We just love to make fun of the rumblings that come out of the mouths of bumbling bureaucrats and public workers who make us wait in line and fill out forms. So in the spirit of finding a funny but stupid statement from a local government office, perhaps nothing beats this expression from Greenville, South Carolina's Department of Social Services: "Your food stamps will be stopped effective March 1992 because we received notice that you passed away. May God bless

you. You may reapply if there is a change in your circum-
stances."

6. IRS TRAINING MANUAL FOR TAX AUDITORS

Yes, it is a true joy to find a stupid expression from a government agency. And when that agency is the IRS, it makes one
want to do cartwheels. When the IRS issued a training man-
ual, it included the following line: "You will find it a distinct
help if you know and look as if you know what you are
doing."

7. VICE PRESIDENT AL GORE'S INVENTION

You've heard this man before. After serving as Bill Clinton's
vice president, he ran for president in 2000. Before that he
didn't say too much. But he may always be remembered for
the infamous words he spoke in a 1999 interview with CNN's
Wolf Blitzer: "During my service in the United States Congress, I took the initiative in creating the Internet."

8. THE NIGERIAN 419 LETTER SCAM

On most any given day, this letter scam is out and about and
is one that federal investigators warn against. (The "419" refers to the Nigerian criminal statute for fraud.) The Nigerian
e-mail scam highlighted by the FBI, FTC, and U.S. Secret
Service involves an unsolicited e-mail that arrives in your
inbox stating that millions of U.S. dollars need to be removed
from Nigeria and you have been selected by government officials, banking officials, or surviving relatives to assist.
Here's an excerpt from it: "But there will be just a few expenses. Naturally, you will be amply rewarded for your assistance by retaining a percentage of the funds transferred;
however, in order to facilitate the procedure your financial
assistance is required up front."

9. *BUSINESS WEEK* MAGAZINE'S FAULTY FORECAST

Automobiles contribute significantly to our Gross National
Product. It wasn't long ago that American companies ruled

the U.S. auto market. But today things are different. To see how different, consider this quote from the August 2, 1968, issue of *Business Week* magazine: "With over 50 foreign cars already on sale here, the Japanese auto industry isn't likely to carve out a big slice of the U.S. market."

10. WESTERN UNION MEMO

Alexander Graham Bell invented the first telephone in 1876, and those "landlines" are now being rapidly replaced by cell phones. Just to show how differently people thought then, consider this quote from an 1876 Western Union memo: "This 'telephone' has too many shortcomings to be seriously considered as a means of communication. The device is inherently of no value to us."

Technology of a Different Color

Technology makes industry grow. No matter what the industry, innovation rises from the great minds beneath it. A great number of African Americans have contributed inventions and technological developments that have shaped many an organization and industry. These innovations have, in turn, affected our everyday lives. Here are some invention stories you may have never heard.[1]

1. DR. MEREDITH GOURDINE (1929–1998), ELECTROGASDYNAMICS

Gourdine attended Cornell University and later earned a PhD in engineering science from the California Institute of Technology, Pasadena. The company he built was founded on the principles of electrogasdynamics (EGD), a way to disperse fog and smoke. Using its principles, he converted natural gas to electricity. Applications for the process include refrigeration, desalination of seawater, and reducing the pollutants in smoke. Gourdine is credited with over forty patents.

[1] Information gathered from www.inventors.about.com/library/blblackinventors.htm.

2. GEORGE WASHINGTON CARVER (1864–1943), SCIENTIST AND AGRICULTURALIST

Carver made notable strides in the agronomy of the southern United States. He redirected the emphasis of southern farming to nitrate-producing crops, such as peanuts, peas, sweet potatoes, pecans, and soybeans, and away from the traditional but risky agricultural pursuit of cotton, which depletes nutrients in the soil. Southern growers began rotating their crops with peanuts followed by cotton. Carver developed over 300 uses for peanuts and 118 products from the sweet potato, two crops that had previously been viewed as being of limited use. Carver also introduced the creation of synthetic marble from sawdust, plastics from wood shavings, and writing paper from wisteria vines.

3. CHARLES DREW (1904–1950), DEVELOPMENTS IN BLOOD AND TECHNOLOGY

While serving as a researcher at New York's Columbia University, Drew discovered that blood could be preserved and reconstituted at a later date. He found that this was possible by separating the liquid red blood cells from the near-solid plasma and freezing the two separately. His processes were used by the British military during World War II in creating mobile blood banks for wounded soldiers. Drew was the first African American to earn a doctor of medical science degree from Columbia.

4. JAN ERNST MATZELIGER (1852–1889), SHOE MANUFACTURING

At the age of eighteen, Matzeliger emigrated from Dutch Guiana and went to work in a shoe factory in Philadelphia. The production of shoes was done by hand, and he revolutionized the shoe industry by introducing a shoe lasting (molding) machine that would fasten a sole to the shoe in one minute. Thus, while previously handmade shoes could be turned out at a rate of 50 pairs per day, Matzeliger's new machine increased production to between 150 to 700 pairs of shoes per day.

5. GARRETT MORGAN (1877-1963), INVENTED A GAS INHALATOR

Form does follow function—well, at least it did for Garrett Morgan. He and a few other volunteers were rescuing a group of men after an explosion in a smoke-filled tunnel under Lake Erie. This rescue earned Morgan a gold medal from the City of Cleveland and the Second International Exposition of Safety and Sanitation in New York. It also gave him the idea for a gas inhalator. The U.S. Army used his device as gas masks for combat troops during World War I. Because he often faced racial prejudice, Morgan had a difficult time introducing his invention. But because of Morgan's innovation, today's firefighters are able to enter dangerous environments without harm from smoke or fumes. Morgan also invented an important improvement to traffic signals and a zigzag attachment to manually operated sewing machines.

6. HENRY GREEN PARKS JR. (1916-1989), SCRAPPLE

"More Parks sausages, Mom, please!" Many remember the advertising tag line and the aroma of sausage and scrapple cooking in kitchens in America. Parks founded the Parks Sausage Company in 1951 and registered several trademarks. The word "please" was added by Parks after many complained that the advertisement conjured up disrespect for Mom. H. G. Parks, Inc., was often listed as one of America's top one hundred African American companies.

7. DENNIS WEATHERBY, AUTOMATIC DISHWASHING DETERGENT

It was Weatherby's innovation and foresight while employed by Procter & Gamble that allowed him to receive a patent for the automatic dishwasher detergent Cascade. He also helped to develop Lemon Liquid Cascade. Weatherby later received his master's degree in chemical engineering from the University of Dayton in 1984 and his PhD from Auburn University in 2001.

8. DR. FRANK CROSSLEY (1925–   ), TITANIUM-BASE ALLOYS

Crossley is a metallurgical pioneer who was educated at the Illinois Institute of Technology in Chicago and later performed research there. In the 1950s, few African Americans were commonly found in the engineering fields, and in fact Crossley was the first African American to receive a doctorate degree in metallurgical engineering. The modest, soft-spoken engineer excelled in his field, earning some seven patents. Five of these involved titanium-base alloys that greatly improved the aircraft and aerospace industry.

9. VALERIE L. THOMAS, ILLUSION TRANSMITTER

After being one of only two women to major in physics in her Morgan State University class, Thomas became a scientist with NASA and later went on to invent the illusion transmitter. Patented in 1980, this device transmits a three-dimensional, real-time image via a cable or electromagnetic means. Thomas's vision was that people would one day be able to watch 3-D projections of their favorite entertainers in their own homes.

10. BENJAMIN BANNEKER (1731–1806), THE FIRST FARMER'S ALMANAC AND THE FIRST STRIKING CLOCK

Considered by some as the first African American scientist, Banneker could hardly be accused of a narrow mind. He was a scientist, astronomer, inventor, writer, and created the first striking clock developed in America. Among his many contributions to the world was the first Farmer's Almanac, titled the *New Jersey, Pennsylvania, Delaware, Maryland, and Virginia Almanac and Ephemeris*, in 1792. Banneker also was an ardent advocate of antislavery and was impressed with Thomas Jefferson in the late 1700s for his keen ability in surveying and mapping.

Ten Economists you Really Should Know About

There is a dearth of economist jokes out there. One goes something like "if you lined up all the economists and strew them out, you'd encircle the globe several times." Any student of business learns certain economic principles in his or her course of study: demand shifts left and supply shifts right, and price is where supply meets demand . . . or something like that. Economics gets complicated, and it's hard to be fully engaged in economic thinking all the time. For career economists, charts, graphs, demand, supply, and a plethora of other measurements are their bread and butter. Here are some economists you really should know something about.

1. JOHN KENNETH GALBRAITH (1908–)

The Canadian-born economist was a professor of economics at Harvard University in 1949 and was viewed as one of the leading economists of the left. He believed in the power of the government to intervene and sponsor large projects for the public good.

2. MILTON FRIEDMAN (1912–)

Friedman won the Nobel Prize for economics and is known for his free market philosophy. He was a monetarist and believed that control of the money supply was important to control the effects of inflation. But as a monetarist, he also believed that control of the money supply was the only intervention that the government should make. Friedman served as economic advisor to two presidents: Richard Nixon and Ronald Reagan.

3. JOHN MAYNARD KEYNES (1883–1946)

A British economist, Keynes advocated intervention of government policy to control and stimulate economic conditions. Study him in an economics course and you'll learn that he wrote *The General Theory of Employment, Interests, and Money* and later built a career on this topic. Perhaps his greatest line was: "In the long run we're all dead."

4. KARL MARX (1818–1883)

He wasn't just an economist but also a political philosopher and social theorist. The world might not have been the same without his influence—for better or for worse. His line "The interests of capitalists and wage-laborers are diametrically opposed to each other" may have been the basis for the formation of many socialist governments. His philosophies revolved around labor and the effect of its production. That said, his theories are long and complicated, and many an economist has dissected his theories and beliefs ad nauseam.

5. JOHN STUART MILL (1806–1873)

Another Brit, Mill was a philosopher and economist. He was a proponent of utilitarianism—a philosophy that seeks to maximize the happiness and welfare ("utility") of the greatest number of people. His economic work, initially based on David Ricardo's theories, generally supported laissez faire policies but also argued that nothing in economics theory precluded an economic order based on socialist principles. He was thought to be a boy genius and read voraciously.

6. ADAM SMITH (1723–1790)

A Scottish economist and philosopher, Smith was the author of the well-hailed *The Wealth of Nations*, which was published in 1776. It has been heralded as one of the most influential economic books in history and is on the reading list of many high flyers in the business community.

7. VILFREDO PARETO (1848–1923)

This Italian philosopher and economist made important contributions to economics. He launched the concepts of efficiency, optimal allocation, distribution, and choice. His teachings helped shape the field of microeconomics. But far and above all of his principles, he is best known for his observation that 20 percent of the population owned 80 percent of the property in his native Italy. Yes, he is the father of the 80–20 rule, which is still alive and well in the world today.

8. JOHN FORBES NASH (1928–   )

Nash is a more contemporary economist. He won the 1994 Nobel Prize in economics, which he shared with two other economists. A mathematician who focused on game theory and geometry, Nash began to suffer from schizophrenia at age thirty. His ability in mathematics was exceptional, and he might well be the first Nobel Prize winner to have suffered from schizophrenia. Nash was a professor at Princeton and later at MIT. He was the subject of the 2001 movie *A Beautiful Mind*.

9. ROBERT SOLOW (1924–   )

Another winner of the Nobel Prize in economics, Solow worked up a theory of economic growth, which became his contribution to the field. His concept, also referred to as the neoclassical growth model, designates three categories of determinants of economic growth: labor, capital, and technological progress. He quantified the effects of the output of the U.S. laborer and determined that about 80 percent of this output was due to technological progress.

10.   JAMES TOBIN (1918–2002)

Tobin was an economic advisor to the John F. Kennedy administration and was also a professor at Yale. A Keynesian,
Tobin believed that governments should intervene in the
economy in order to stabilize output and avoid recessions.
One of his most notable claims to fame was his proposed tax
on foreign exchange transactions. This tax would regulate
currency speculation and could help fund Third World development or UN activity.

The Southpaws

There's no doubt about it. We live in a right-handed world. It is said that only about 10 percent of the world's population is left-handed. Interestingly, the right side of the brain controls the left hand. The right side of the brain also has a great influence on our sense of visual and spatial relations, creativity, and nonverbal thinking. Could this be the reason that many a famous visionary is left-handed?

It's not easy to find an expert to agree with this theory, but for what it's worth, many great achievers were left-handed. Here are some of note.[1]

1. HENRY FORD (1863–1947)

The tough, adamant automaker was influenced by scientific management and was the first to conceive of his automaking business as a scientific endeavor with a production line that could crank out units. His Model T provided the highways with a new mode of transportation. He was a tough boss, but paid his workers well and strove to build the best. He made a successful mark on American industry and he was left-handed.

[1] Information gathered from www.anythinglefthanded.co.uk.

2. DAVID ROCKEFELLER (1915–)

This famous name of the banking world has a long history of forming advisory boards about banking and bucks. What most people know about him is that he is quite a philanthropist and created large endowments for scientific and medical research, founding organizations such as Rockefeller University in New York. But there are two bits of information that most people don't know about David Rockefeller: he collected beetles, and he is left-handed.

3. BILL GATES (1955–)

The six-foot, six-inch titan may have created the Microsoft empire, but he didn't do it with his right hand. Although Bill Gates is a southpaw, the majority of Microsoft equipment is for right-handed users, probably because 90 percent of the world population is right-handed.

4. H. ROSS PEROT (1930–)

This former Eagle Scout, Naval Academy graduate, and quick-talking whipper-snapper just may be the reason that Bill Clinton got elected. His ambition led him not only to run for president in 1992 and 1996, but also to found EDS, a computer consultancy, which grew to be a major player in the information technology industry. He likes sharply pressed suits, crew cuts, and pie charts, and he is left-handed.

5. LEONARDO DA VINCI (1452–1519)

An interesting figure in world history, da Vinci redefines the idea of a well-rounded individual. He was able to write in mirror image and wrote pages of prose and text in such a manner. His ability to visualize led him to the earliest sketches of things such as helicopters and engineering innovations that would become legendary in centuries to come. Perhaps his most notable accomplishment was his artistic creations as an Italian painter.

6. ALBERT EINSTEIN (1879–1955)

This Nobel Prize–winning scientist would come to conceive the theory of relativity after years of research and trial in the scientific community. He worked as a technical examiner at a patent office in Switzerland, was a researcher at Princeton University, and was instrumental in the development of atomic power.

7. BENJAMIN FRANKLIN (1706–1790)

If it weren't for Ben Franklin and his kite, we might not have lights in our homes today. Ben Franklin contributed so many concepts, ideas, and innovations to the development of our nation, it would take a thick volume to discuss them all. He was a statesman, merchant, printer, and inventor, and like so many other great achievers, he was left-handed.

8. SIR ISAAC NEWTON (1642–1727)

This early mathematician and scientist gave us the principle of gravity among other findings in his bag of scientific discovery. He viewed everything from a mathematical stance and used calculations to predict and explain. He also served several years as a Member of Parliament and as Master of the Royal Mint.

9. LOU GERSTNER (1942–   )

Before serving as the CEO of IBM, Gerstner worked with RJR Nabisco and American Express. Following in the footsteps of Thomas Watson and the traditions of Big Blue is no easy feat, but Gerstner did so from 1993 until March 2002. In January 2003 he assumed the position of chairman at the Carlyle Group in Washington, D.C. If you happen to notice Gerstner sitting at his desk, writing out a big fat check, you may notice that he does so with his left hand.

10. RANSOM E. OLDS (1864–1950)

R. E. Olds was the founder of the Olds Motor Vehicle Company in 1897 and later the REO Motor Company. An inventor and innovator of the internal combustion engine, Olds came from Geneva, Ohio, and developed an inexpensive but stylish vehicle that was one of the first to be made in quantity. He turned to making lawn mower engines after the car market softened and continued to dabble in different speculative endeavors. For what it's worth, he was left-handed.

The Long Gray Line

The tradition at the United States Military Academy at West Point has always been one of valor, courage, duty, and honor. In addition to producing great military leaders, the academy produced some of the most lauded achievers in government and industry. Specifically, West Point graduates have risen to the top ranks of American entities of enterprise. Here are some notable corporate leaders who were educated at the United States Military Academy.[1]

1. JOHN G. HAYES

John Hayes was a member of West Point's class of 1949. His academic and leadership training led him to the post as president of the Coca-Cola Bottling Company.

2. WILLIAM T. SEAWELL (1918–   )

William Seawell was a member of West Point's class of 1941. His military background and training and later experience as a military officer pushed him through the corporate ranks to

[1] Information gathered from www.west-point.org/users/usma1989/
46256.grads.htm.

become chairman of the board and chief executive officer for
Pan Am World Airways.

3. REUBEN POMERANTZ (1921–1993)

Reuben Pomerantz was a member of the U.S. Military Academy at West Point's class of 1946. His training and experience gave him the necessary background to become
president of Holiday Inns of America.

4. RANDOLPH ARASKOG

Randolph Araskog was a member of West Point's class of
1953. Araskog became president and chairman of the IT&T
Corporation.

5. PETER M. DAWKINS (1938–   )

Pete Dawkins was at West Point at a time when another West
Point graduate, Dwight D. Eisenhower, was president of the
United States. Dawkins was a member of West Point's class
of 1959. His football ability landed him the prestigious Heisman Trophy. His skill and leadership launched him into the
position of vice chairman of Citibank and later chairman and
CEO of Primerica Corporation.

6. OMAR N. BRADLEY (1893–1981)

Here's a name you may recognize even if you never knew he
became a business leader. Omar Bradley was a member of
West Point's class of 1915. Two fighting vehicles are named
after this five-star general, and his name can be found in
most textbooks on American history for his role as com-
mander of the 1st Army in World War II. He was also the
army's chief of staff and was the first chairman of the U.S.
Joint Chiefs of Staff, from 1949 to 1953. He headed the U.S.
Veterans Administration and later became chairman of the
board of the Bulova Watch Company in 1958.

7. ALEXANDER M. HAIG JR. (1924–   )

Alexander Haig was a member of West Point's class of 1947.
He is another West Point graduate and is most recognizable

for his later role as White House chief of staff after Richard Nixon resigned from the presidency in 1974. He had served a combat tour from 1966 to 1967 in Vietnam. He was later the secretary of state under President Reagan. It is rumored that Haig was the figure nicknamed "Deep Throat" who gave information to the *Washington Post* after the infamous Watergate break-in. He was also the president and chief operating officer of United Technologies from 1979 to 1981.

8. FRANK BORMAN (1928–   )

Frank Borman was a member of West Point's class of 1950. Like several other classmates, Borman took his leadership skills into the air. He was an astronaut on Gemini 7 in 1965 and on Apollo 8 in 1968. After retiring from NASA and the air force, Borman joined Eastern Airlines and rose to become its CEO in 1975.

9. JAMES KIMSEY (1939–   )

James Kimsey was a member of West Point's class of 1962. Kimsey was a U.S. Army airborne ranger and later served in Vietnam. He was an entrepreneur who founded and invested in restaurants, information technology, and real estate, among other interests. In 1985 Kimsey founded Quantum Computer Services, where he signed up Steve Case to help run the company. In 1990 the company changed its name to America Online, Incorporated. He remains chairman emeritus of the firm and also heads the America Online Foundation.

10. HENRY A. DUPONT (1838–1926)

DuPont graduated first in West Point's class of 1861. Upon graduation he joined the Union Army and eventually achieved the rank of first lieutenant in the 5th Regiment, U.S. Artillery. DuPont remained in the army until 1875, reaching the rank of lieutenant colonel, and received the Congressional Medal of Honor for his role in the battle of Cedar

Creek. After his military career, he became the president of the Wilmington and Western Railroad, and from 1905 to 1917 he served as a Delaware senator. Though he was born into the opulence of the DuPonts of Delaware, he never entered into their chemical operations.

White-Collar Criminals You May Never Forget

M any notorious white-collar crimes have taken place in the business world. What's interesting about such crimes is that the majority have occurred within the last fifty years, and as each year goes by, notorious white-collar criminals become more and more commonplace. Here are some you may just never forget.

1. JEFFERY SKILLING (1953–), THE ENRON SCANDAL

Thousands of people lost their pensions and life savings in 2001 when the Enron Corporation allegedly cooked its books and subsequently acknowledged more than $1 billion in previously undisclosed liabilities. Skilling was chief executive officer and spoke with zeal and vision. The charisma of this Harvard graduate and McKinsey alumnus enticed many to believe that Enron was out to become a global leader in a free market.

2. CHARLES PONZI (1882–1949), THE PONZI SCHEME

This plan in the early 1900s involved the arbitrage of postal coupons. Charles Ponzi attempted to buy them from Spain and sell them to the U.S. Postal Service to take advantage of a price discrepancy between the two rates. His crime was magnified when he raised capital by wooing investors into a promise of a 50 percent return in just ninety days. He went to the slammer for jilting some 40,000 people out of nearly $15 million.

3.　SAM WAKSAL (1947–　), IMCLONE SYSTEMS

In 2002 Waksal pleaded guilty to unloading stock in his research firm, ImClone Systems, before news of a negative FDA ruling became public. Waksal was sentenced to several years in prison. What made the incident so notable and memorable was the alleged tip-off of his friend Martha Stewart, the pinup girl of home décor.

4.　ALBERT J. DUNLAP, SUNBEAM CORPORATION

Dunlap may be best known as "Chainsaw Al" for his renegade style of cutting heads and laying off thousands and thousands of people inside the organizations he was brought in to clean out. The West Point graduate talked a tough talk that was at one time highly respected and drove the stock price of several companies upward under his reign. It all ended when the board at Sunbeam gave ol' Chainsaw Al a taste of the hair of the dog that bit thousands of laid-off employees and they axed Dunlap himself. The crime: fabrication of earnings and revenues that many said was common practice for Dunlap.

5.　IVAN BOESKY (1937–　) AND MICHAEL MILKEN (1946–　), DREXEL BURNHAM LAMBERT

These two hotshots from the now-defunct Drexel Burnham Lambert gave insider trading a whole new look—one that is looked down upon, that is. In 1986 they were tried for market manipulation, and Milken's testimony helped convict Boesky. Both served prison terms, though many felt the terms were too short: Milken served twenty-four months, and Boesky served twenty-two months.

6. BERNIE EBBERS (1941–   ), WORLDCOM

Ebbers and his zealous charge to build a long distance empire after deregulation put credence into the axiom that power corrupts. Ebbers was charged with a $9 billion accounting scandal that led to the telecommunications company's bankruptcy in 2002. He was yet another criminal in the era of uncovering, which seemed to gain newfound momentum in the late 1990s and beyond.

7. IRWIN H. "SONNY" BLOCH, RADIO TALK SHOW HOST AND AUTHOR OF PERSONAL FINANCE BOOKS

Sonny Bloch was charged with securities fraud for representing his sponsors of wireless cable and radio ventures on a nationally syndicated radio program, "The Sonny Bloch Show." Bloch had 1.5 million listeners and a good reputation as a consumer advocate. He agreed to endorse the sale of the risky limited partnerships. He vouched for the character of the promoters and the financial soundness of the ventures on his radio program. Despite the fact that Bloch was paid $2,000 per week for these endorsements, he made them sound personal rather than commercial. The conspirators used Bloch's radio program to develop leads to market their ventures. Sonny Bloch pleaded guilty to eight of the thirty-five counts in the indictment on September 18, 1996, for taking payments from the sponsors for touting worthless securities. He was ordered to pay $5.2 million in restitution and died of lung cancer while in prison.

8. WADE COOK (1949–   ), PERSONAL FINANCE INFOMERCIAL SALESMAN AND SUPPOSED EXPERT

Cook's fast-talking radio advertisements, tape series, expensive seminars, and self-published books attracted thousands of vulnerable prospects in search of the quick, easy buck. But the quick, easy buck really ended up going to Cook. He was sued in several states on numerous charges for exaggerating facts, over-promising returns, and under-delivering on his promises. In 2000 the Federal Trade Commission held Cook personally responsible for an estimated $1.5 million in claims not paid to consumers under the settlement of another suit.

9. BILLIE SOL ESTES (1924–   ), MANIPULATOR OF THE WEST TEXAS FERTILIZER MARKET

The man who now calls himself the King of the Texas Wheeler-Dealers built up capital by mortgaging close to $200 million dollars of nonexistent farm gear. He was jailed in 1965 and was paroled in 1971. If the road to recovery is ever marred by relapse, Estes seemed to exemplify it. He again tried to mortgage things, but this time it was nonexistent oil equipment rather than farm gear, and he was subsequently given a five-year prison term. Among his many ties to criminal activities, Estes claims to know who shot President John F. Kennedy.

10. MARC RICH (1934–   ), FRAUDULENT OIL TRADES

Rich and his partner, Pinky Green, engaged in fraudulent oil trading in the 1980–1981 time frame. They moved the cash netted to offshore subsidiaries and ran away to Switzerland, fearing the hammer of New York's mayor, Rudolph Giuliani. In 1983, Rich was indicted for tax evasion in the amount of more than $48 million. He was also charged with tax fraud and with running illegal oil deals with Iran. Some guys get all the breaks, and the two proved it when, in a controversial decision, President Clinton pardoned Rich and Green in 2001.

Good Fellows Club

The White House Fellow—it's one of the most prestigious selections that an emerging leader can experience. The program was initiated by President Lyndon B. Johnson in 1964. White House Fellows undergo a rigid and competitive selection process, and the eleven to nineteen candidates who are chosen then spend a period of time in and around Washington, the president, and government. The end result is that they become great leaders. Many of them turn to industry and nonprofit organizations to lead and manage. Here are the names of ten White House Fellows, with the year of their fellowship and the organization they went on to lead.[1]

1. **GARREY E. CARRUTHERS (1939–)**

President/CEO, Cimarron Health Plan; former governor of New Mexico. Carruthers served as a White House Fellow from 1974 to 1975.

2. **MARSHALL N. CARTER (1940–)**

Former chairman/CEO, State Street Bank & Trust Corporation. A West Point graduate and former Marine Corps officer, Carter served as a White House Fellow from 1975 to 1976.

[1] Information gathered from www.whitehouse.gov/fellows.

3. PETER M. DAWKINS (1938–   )

Chairman/CEO, Diversified Distribution Services, The Travelers Group; brigadier general, U.S. Army (ret.); former chairman/CEO, Primerica Financial Services, Inc.; 1958 Heisman Trophy winner. Dawkins served as a White House Fellow from 1973 to 1974.

4. MARSHA J. EVANS (1948–   )

President/CEO of American Red Cross; former national executive director, Girl Scouts of America. Evans served as a White House Fellow from 1979 to 1980.

5. ELAINE L. CHAO (1953–   )

Secretary of Labor under President George W. Bush; former president/CEO, United Way of America; former director, Peace Corps; Heritage Foundation scholar. Chao served as a White House Fellow from 1983 to 1984.

6. MYRON E. ULLMAN III (1947–   )

CEO, J. C. Penney; former CEO, LVMH Moet Hennessy Louis Vuitton; former chairman/CEO, DFS Group, LTD; former chairman/CEO, R. H. Macy Company. Ullman served as a White House Fellow from 1981 to 1982.

7. LUIS G. NOGALES

President, Nogales Partners; former chairman/CEO, United Press International; former president, Univision. Nogales served as a White House Fellow from 1972 to 1973.

8. DANA G. MEAD (1936–   )

Former chairman/CEO, Tenneco, Inc.; chairman, MIT Corporation. Mead served as a White House Fellow from 1970 to 1971.

9. **TOM JOHNSON (1942–   )**

Former chairman/CEO, CNN; former publisher/CEO, *Los Angeles Times*. Johnson served as a White House Fellow from 1965 to 1966.

10. **ROBERT D. HAAS (1943–   )**

Chairman/CEO, Levi Strauss. Haas served as a White House Fellow from 1968 to 1969.

Female Edisons

Innovation is paramount to success in most avenues of business, and almost every school kid alive gets some education in the story behind some of the world's most famous inventions from people like Eli Whitney, Thomas Edison, and Cyrus McCormick. But not everyone learns the stories of some of the unsung *female* heroes of invention. Here is a list of women whose inventions may sound off the beaten path but nevertheless have made life much easier.[1]

1. SARAH MATHER, THE SUBMARINE TELESCOPE AND LAMP

If there's ever a tidbit of trivia that you can impress your friends with, this may be it: in 1845 Sarah Mather received a patent for the invention of a submarine telescope and lamp. This is a bit different from the periscope, which allowed submarines to survey surrounding ships and vessels. This device permitted seagoing vessels to survey the depths of the ocean. Ironically, the U.S. Navy's submarine corps is one of the few branches of the armed services in which women are not allowed to participate.

[1] Information gathered from www.uspto.gov/go/kids/ponder8.htm.

2. STEPHANIE LOUISE KWOLEK (1923–   ), KEVLAR

You probably should be more thankful to Kwolek than you know. Kwolek's research for the DuPont Company led to the development of a synthetic material called Kevlar. This material is five times stronger than the same mass of steel. Patented by Kwolek in 1966, Kevlar does not rust or corrode and is extremely lightweight. The material is used in bulletproof vests, underwater cables, brake linings, airplane windshields, football helmets, space vehicles, boats, parachutes, skis, and building materials.

3. MARTHA J. COSTON (1826–1902), THE PYROTECHNIC FLARE

Coston was married to a naval scientist who, before his death, had made a rough sketch in a diary for pyrotechnic flares. After his passing, his wife took over the idea and developed an innovation called Night Signals. These enabled ships to communicate messages despite darkness. The U.S. Navy purchased the patent rights, and these flares were the basis of a system of communication that helped save lives and win battles.

4. MARGARET KNIGHT (1838–1914), STOP-MOTION DEVICE

Knight received her first patent at the age of thirty, though her innovative quest began much earlier when she made sleds and kites for her brothers while growing up in Maine. At age twelve she had an idea for a device that could be used in textile mills to shut down machinery based on motion. Such a device would keep workers from injury. She would go on to earn some twenty-six patents, including one for a machine that made flat-bottomed paper bags that is still used to this very day!

5. SUSAN TAYLOR CONVERSE, ONE-PIECE FLANNEL EMANCIPATION SUIT

In Converse's day, women's undergarments included tight corsets. It was an uncomfortable sight for any casual observer. Consequently, women's groups throughout the nation felt that less restrictive underclothing made sense. In 1875 Converse designed a one-piece garment with no bones, eyelets, or laces called the "Union Under-Flannel," which was well received and quite successful.

6. KATHERINE BLODGETT (1898–1979), THE WORLD'S FIRST 100 PERCENT TRANSPARENT OR INVISIBLE GLASS

Blodgett was the first female scientist hired by General Electric's Research Laboratory in Schenectady, New York. She was also the first woman to earn a PhD in physics from Cambridge University. She won a Nobel Prize for coatings technology and later discovered a way to apply the coatings layer-by-layer to glass and metal. Such thin films reduced glare on reflective surfaces when layered to a certain thickness, and would block the reflection from the surface underneath. This became known as the world's first 100 percent transparent or invisible glass. This technology was used for antireflective coatings in eyeglasses, microscopes, telescopes, and camera and projector lenses.

7. JULIE NEWMAR (1935–   ), ULTRA-SHEER, ULTRA-SNUG PANTYHOSE

Although nylon stockings had been around since 1940, pantyhose were not developed until 1959. And in 1977 actress Julie Newmar patented "Nudemar," a new ultra-sheer "pantyhose with shaping band for Cheeky derriere relief."[2] You may better recognize Newmar as the former Catwoman in the TV series *Batman*, or as Rhoda the robot in *My Living Doll*. In addition to her television work, she also made regular appearances on Broadway and in films such as *Seven Brides for Seven Brothers*, *Slaves of Babylon*, and *Mackenna's Gold*.

8. ANN MOORE (1940–   ), THE SNUGLI

Ann Moore was a Peace Corps volunteer who observed mothers in French West Africa carrying their babies securely

[2] Quote found on the Internet Movie Database, www.imdb.com.

on their backs. Such observation led her to admire the bonding between the African mother and child. When she later returned home to the United States and had her own baby, Moore and her mother designed a carrier for Moore's daughter similar to those she had seen abroad. Moore and her husband began to market the carrier, called the Snugli, which offers comfort and convenience for parents and their babies the world over.

9. BETTE NESMITH GRAHAM (1924–1980), LIQUID PAPER

If you've ever relied on the typewriter for written correspondence, your life may have been made a tad easier by the works of this woman. A secretary and aspiring artist, Graham used her own kitchen blender to invent Liquid Paper (originally called "Mistake Out"), the first typing correction fluid. As a side note, Nesmith is the mother of Mike Nesmith of the music group and eponymous television show *The Monkees*.

10. RUTH HANDLER (1916–2002), THE BARBIE DOLL

Handler was one of the original founders of Mattel, Inc. The Barbie doll was originally created in 1965 with bendable legs. The doll was named after Handler's own daughter, which was different in the sense that earlier dolls were named after storybook characters and figures. Here was a doll named after a real-life teenage girl. Though her measurements, if scaled to human size, would be an impossible 36-18-38, Barbie has sold widely and can be found in many young girls' rooms.

A Few Words about Wealth, Money, and Power

W hat do they say about money and power? Well, it just depends on who you talk to. Throughout history we've looked at money and power from every conceivable angle. It seems that money and power move us in a different way than do other things and, as such, they have led people to have different perspectives on this topic. Here are a few thoughts from some people with a good deal of experience on the subject.[1]

1. **ALBERT EINSTEIN (1879–1955)**

If you think taxes are a difficult thing to understand, you're not alone. Our own Albert Einstein could pull the gray hair out of his head in trying to do his own taxes. In fact, Ronald Reagan utilized Einstein's views when he was introducing reasons for his tax reforms. It was Einstein who said: "The hardest thing in the world to understand is income tax."

2. **J. PAUL GETTY (1892–1976)**

Getty's fortune is one that has been the source of many great art collections. His philanthropic side came out when he

[1] Quotes from www.taxgaga.com, www.brainyquote.com, www.born tomotivate.com, and www.spicyquotes.com.

said: "Money is like manure. You have to spread it around or it smells."

3. ANDREW CARNEGIE (1835–1919)

Carnegie was a man of distinct business philosophy. He believed that wealth followed a certain pattern of behavior and principle. That may be why he stated: "Mr. Morgan buys his partners. I grow my own."

4. WINSTON CHURCHILL (1874–1965)

Winston Churchill, who suffered from severe dyslexia, depression, and some may say diplomacy, was a shrewd master of oratory and good sense. He extolled the virtue of a capitalist state by saying: "It is a socialist idea that making profits is a vice. I consider the real vice is making losses."

5. FRANK W. WOOLWORTH (1852–1919)

Woolworth played to the opposite of many fortune seekers. Instead of going after the mother lode of riches, he went after the nickels and dimes of the working class by creating a string of stores with inexpensively priced goods, saying: "I am the world's worst salesman; therefore, I must make it easy for people to buy."

6. BERNARD BARUCH (1870–1965)

Oh, the many stock market pundits who only wish their fortune came in the same magnitude as Baruch's. Baruch explained the simplicity and common sense of his approach to the stock market when he said: "Repeatedly in my market operations, I have sold a stock while it was rising—and that has been one reason I have held on to my fortune."

7. DONALD T. REGAN (1818–2003)

Former treasury secretary and White House chief of staff Donald T. Regan was a leader on Wall Street who had something to say about monetary policy and the how and what of market dynamics. This was illustrated in his quote: "Many

Wall Street firms have what they call a structure, but which more closely resembles a scaffold."

8. JOHN D. ROCKEFELLER (1839–1937)

John D. Rockefeller took pleasure in life's simple things. To him, this revolved around watching the dividend income stream in from his colossal investments. He spoke his mind when he said: "Do you know the only thing that gives me pleasure? It is to see my dividends coming in."

9. JOHN F. KENNEDY (1917–1963)

John F. Kennedy came from a family that knew the inner mind of the capitalist. His father was a wealthy man and was successful at several business ventures. Speaking to staff members about steel industry executives who increased prices, the former president said: "My father always told me that all businessmen were sons of bitches but I never believed it till now."

10. BENJAMIN FRANKLIN (1706–1790)

The simple wisdom of our own Benjamin Franklin is immortal. His words will endure forever. And he taught us so much about money when he said: "If you would like to know the value of money, go and try to borrow some."

The Under-Forty Set

Anyone who believes that youth is wasted on the young may not realize that there are a number of businessmen who founded their ventures before the age of forty. Here are some who did just that.

1. EUGENE MCDONALD (1886–1958)

After hearing his first radio broadcast on New Year's Eve in 1920, McDonald developed a fascination with the medium and founded the Zenith Corporation at age thirty-seven. Mc-Donald took advantage of the emergence of radio broadcasting in the early 1920s, when personalities like "The Lone Ranger" and Jack Benny first became household names. He is credited with introducing the first portable radio in 1924.

2. CHARLES PFIZER (1824–1906)

Chemist Charles Pfizer founded Pfizer Pharmaceuticals at the age of twenty-eight. He began his firm in the mid-1800s by producing pharmaceutical products that weren't available in the United States at the time. One of his first products was santonin, created to treat parasitic worms. He also found a way to manufacture citric acid, used to flavor many of today's foods. The company began its operation in New York City and has remained there ever since.

3. J. WILLARD MARRIOTT (1900–1985)

He founded the Marriott Corporation at the age of twenty-six. The company actually began as an A&W Root Beer stand in 1928. The former naval supply officer also built "Hot Shoppes" during the war years. They were built on a sixteen-hour-a-day operation and were the closest thing to fast food at the time. The first Marriott hotel was opened in 1957, in Washington, D.C.

4. DONALD W. DOUGLAS (1892–1981)

Although he preferred sailing to flying, Donald Douglas founded the Douglas Aircraft Corporation at the age of twenty-eight. One of history's first aeronautical engineers, his original intent was to build aircraft capable of flying non-stop across America. The business flourished in the early 1920s and took off with several navy contracts, from which it has built its niche as a major defense contractor.

5. GEORGE WESTINGHOUSE (1846–1914)

Receiving his first patent at the age of nineteen, George Westinghouse was one of the nation's most prolific inventors. He not only invented compressed-air brakes for trains at the age of twenty-two, he also founded the Westinghouse Electric Corporation at the age of thirty-nine. After purchasing patent rights from Nikola Tesla, Westinghouse brought forth alternating current (AC) power. This form of power was able to allow a central source of power, giving way to the utility industry and its supply of electricity to the masses.

6. WILLIAM R. HEWLETT (1913–2001) AND DAVID PACKARD (1912–1996)

These two Stanford University graduates founded the Hewlett-Packard Company in 1939, when they were both twenty-six. They started their work in Packard's garage with a mere

$538 in start-up capital. Originally the partners had grand ideas that revolved around their electrical engineering savvy and designing and marketing electrical gizmos and devices. The late 1930s brought in contract engineering jobs whereby the firm farmed out their engineering intellect. They later sold some oscilloscopes and eventually got on track during the war years when the company started to grow.

7. JOHN W. NORDSTROM (1871–1963)

A Swedish immigrant, John Nordstrom immigrated to the United States in 1887 and made his way to Seattle, where he eventually founded what later became Nordstrom's department store. In the early part of the twentieth century, Nordstrom searched for an enterprise to fulfill his entrepreneurial quest. He teamed up with shoemaker Carl Wallin and began a partnership selling shoes under the name Wallin & Nordstrom. John Nordstrom sold out his share of the business to his sons in 1928. Wallin sold his shares to them in 1929, and the two renamed the store Nordstrom's.

8. WILLIAM COLGATE (1783–1857)

In 1806 Colgate founded the Colgate Corporation (later the Colgate-Palmolive Co.) at age twenty-three. In the early 1800s most consumer soap was made at home, and Colgate went after that niche after beginning his career as a soap-maker's apprentice. His pursuit expanded and his products remain a part of many households throughout the world.

9. RICHARD J. REYNOLDS (1850–1918)

Reynolds founded R. J. Reynolds Corporation at age twenty-five. In the post–Civil War era, Reynolds set out to produce and market the finest chewing tobacco. By the late 1800s Reynolds's chewing tobacco was in high demand. The firm entered the twentieth century with smoking tobacco products. Their infamous Camel brand became the number one-selling cigarette in the early 1900s, and the brand's sales in-

creased even more after Reynolds gave them away for free
to World War I soldiers.

10. **MASARU IBUKA (1908–1997)**

Ibuka founded the Sony Corporation at age thirty-seven. You
may think that the electronics giant always had it easy.
Think again. Originally Ibuka launched a flurry of failed
products, including taping devices, rice cookers, and other
paraphernalia. The enterprise stayed afloat by making in-
struments and devices on contract for the Japan Broadcasting Corporation. The company grew slowly and waited
nearly fifteen years until it had its first big hit with a pocket
radio in 1955.

THE PRODUCTS

Dot-com Bombs to Tell Your Children About

There may have been nothing else quite like it. The dot-com craze was on and off in about the course of two years. It was a cultural phenomenon for the many who launched and ran with what they thought was the next big deal for the world of commerce. It's now compared to other big bubble bursts like the Dutch tulip bulb flop and other far-flung dreams and well-planned schemes. Something like 20 percent of the 1,800 plus firms that were dot-com start-ups went under. Here are a few to remember and tell your children about.

1. **BROADCAST.COM**

In their heyday they sold themselves as the mega-site of broadcasting, a one-stop superstore to link to radio stations, audio books, streaming video, and everything you'd ever need to have Webcasts right on your very own computer. Well, the best-laid plans of mice and men often go awry, and broadcast.com did a broadcast belly flop into bankruptcy and found its way right into the dot-com graveyard.

2. **ETOYS.COM**

During the holiday toy blitz, eToys didn't get little Johnny's Rescue Hero there by Christmas Eve. As a result, the company had to give away the store to compensate for its logistical nightmares. It just couldn't cut it as an online toy retailer and, to the dismay of many a bright and shining toy-loving face, filed for bankruptcy in March 2001. KB Toys later purchased the eToys inventory and reopened the Web site. When the new owner itself went under, the dot-com received additional funding and is now back in operation as eToys Direct.

3. PETS.COM

Our pets are like people, but Pets.com which strategically sold everything from dog food to cat balls with bells in them, had to treat their people—the way a failed company does. The company enthusiastically set out in the market with the ideas that people will spend money on their pets, much of the merchandise for pets is a repeat purchase (e.g., food), and the online store makes it convenient and easy. Unfortunately, overspending in marketing efforts and a lack of profits contributed to this dot-com company's demise.

4. MOTHERNATURE.COM

The nutrition business may be big business, but not online, not for this company. The dot-com firm sold vitamins, supplements, and minerals, as well as other products you might find in a health food store. What's good for the body isn't always good for business, and this firm proved it when they took the ultimate nosedive into bankruptcy in 2000. Like many previous dot-com failures, Mothernature.com was reborn in 2002.

5. EGGHEAD.COM

Egghead offered a wide array of products with a large selection in the consumer electronics category. They offered many closeouts and rock-bottom deals; however, the company itself hit rock bottom in 2001 when it went under to the great graveyard for dot-com companies. Egghead.com was later resurrected when it was taken over by Amazon.com, which has rescued other dot-com failures as well.

6. EXCITEHOME.COM

At one time (not so long ago) this firm was a major portal, with games, search engines, e-mail, high-speed broadband Internet access, and the like. It looked like an enterprising, established dot-com player, but it soon became a dot-com skeleton when it went bust in 2001. Excite.com, however, was revamped and is back!

7. GARDEN.COM

The company based in Austin, Texas, had some bright and shining whipper-snappers behind it. They attempted to sell online everything a garden lover could ever want. But Garden.com just couldn't hack it and threw in the towel sometime around 2000. The company was later acquired and revitalized by Wal-Mart and the Burpee company.

8. FURNITURE.COM

Furniture was it. Everybody needs it. Everybody buys it. That was the thrust behind the idea of having an online show-room of furniture. What the creators seemed to overlook was that most people like to sit on it, lay on it, and try it out before they buy, which they couldn't exactly do online. Despite receiving heavy traffic and a $27 million investment from an Internet venture firm, Furniture.com died with so many others in the gloom-and-doom year of 2000. Nevertheless, the site reemerged in 2002 after new ownership took over and a new business model was developed. Although there is a furniture.com today, the original venture failed.

9. VALUE AMERICA

An online merchandise retailer may well exemplify the pursuit of the quick, easy dollar. Backed by some big names at places like Federal Express and Microsoft, when this early-stage, high-technology venture capital company went public, its stock price tripled its first day out of the starting gate. Many criticize the firm's founder and CEO for spending too much on his Virginia estate and corporate jet instead of worrying about the nitty-gritty of making the dot-com a success. Although it helped to establish several dot-com businesses, the company flopped around the year 2000.

10. BOO.COM

The UK-based clothing retailer began online a bit later than its peers, in late 1999. It was unusual in that it began operations in six different countries on the same day. This meant multiple currencies and quite a complex and intricate operation for a dot-com company. The company, which ended up being Europe's first dot-com failure, spent some $65 million in advertising its first year but after only eighteen months, it joined a host of other e-tailers that went flat bust sometime around mid-2000. Although most of the company's assets were purchased by Fashionmall.com, which is still in operation, Boo.com was one of three companies accused of violating privacy agreements by selling the private information of its customers. The domain name is still in operation; however, the original venture failed.

Innovation Creations

"What's good for General Motors is good for the rest of the nation" used to be a phrase that politicians and union leaders would throw around to illustrate our reliance on big business. As the corporation goes, so goes society. Well, when it comes to innovations that affect our daily lives, this is very true. Some of the greatest innovations that we know and use every day come from developments by pioneers within industries. Here are some innovations that have changed our lives, for better or for worse.[1]

1. THE MICROWAVE OVEN (1946)

It was discovered by accident, and don't you just love it? During a radar-related research project in 1946, a Raytheon engineer named Dr. Percy Spencer was testing a new vacuum tube called a magnetron when he noticed that the candy bar in his pocket had melted. The microwaves were then used to pop popcorn and cook an egg. This technology was harnessed to create the first microwave oven, which was nearly 6 feet tall and weighed 750 pounds.

[1] Information gathered from www.inventors.about.com/library.

2. THE FIRST BANK CREDIT CARD (1958)

Sears has been granting credit since about 1910. By the late 1950s, many Americans had a credit card of some kind. In 1958, however, it was Bank of America that first sold and nationally licensed the concept of a loan by using a credit card. Voila! The age of debt was born. Who could live without it today?

3. VALIUM (1963)

The drug's name is derived from Latin, meaning "to be strong and well." Valium was first introduced by Roche Labs in 1963 and became popularized by Mick Jagger and the Rolling Stones as the "little yellow pill" that served as "mother's little helper." The mind-calming drug was the most prescribed drug in the United States during the rough-and-tumble 1970s.

4. AIR CONDITIONING (1902)

It's hard to imagine life without being able to step into a comfortably cool room on a sweltering hot day. Willis Carrier's "apparatus for treating air" was a way to achieve temperature and humidity, thereby "conditioning" the air. Cooling for residential homes began in 1928. Summers would be unbearable without it.

5. THE SINGLE-CHIP MICROPROCESSOR (1971)

In 1971 Intel created a small chip that contained the electronic ingredients for transistor switches to operate on a single processing unit. Without getting too technical, this meant that electronic pulses could happen faster than lightning, and so could computing. While it sounds rather mundane, this innovation has probably influenced our daily life like no other. If it doesn't say "Intel Inside," let the buyer beware.

6. GUNPOWDER (1802)

After studying the production of explosives in his native France, Eleuthère Irénée duPont, a French immigrant, arrived in America in 1800, only to learn of the country's poor quality gunpowder. The young chemist started a saltpeter mill in 1802 on the Brandywine River, and by 1810 he was operating America's largest black-powder plant. One thing led to another and his company sprouted to blue-chip status.

7. POST-IT NOTES (1977)

Go ahead and admit it—you manage some part of your life with them. It was the innovation of one 3M employee, Art Fry, who needed the impossible for his church hymnal: a note tab that would permanently adhere to the page but wouldn't flake away either. After some snooping at his 3M workplace, he found an adhesive, developed by Dr. Spencer Silver, that allowed the form of such notes to follow his function. His problem was solved and "little Post-its" began to take over.

8. TUPPERWARE (1947)

Sooner or later, everyone owns Tupperware. Earl Tupper, a tree surgeon (yes, a guy who cuts down trees), tinkered with plastics in his spare time and used polyethylene to make a plastic container with an airtight lid. But this wasn't the most innovative part of him and the company he founded. The true innovation was the world-famous Tupperware party, which he pioneered himself as the way to market. While his product is a mainstay in our life, the Tupperware party is more so. Today, a Tupperware demonstration begins somewhere in the world approximately every two seconds, with yearly net sales exceeding $1.2 billion.

9. DEODORANTS (1952)

Bristol Myers didn't develop the formula but rather the marketing effort to introduce Ban Roll-On deodorant in 1952. Its earliest ads read "roll on Ban, roll out doubt." And millions of Americans did just that. The product operated under the same principles as another innovation: the ballpoint pen. It wasn't until 1965 that Bristol Myers really began to make

serious progress with a spin off of Ban Roll-On: aerosol deodorant.

10. **JAVA (1990)**

You probably have heard about it but don't know exactly
what it is. (No, it's not a reference to coffee). Java is a programming language and environment invented by James
Gosling in 1994 while he worked on the Green Project at the
Silicon Valley–based Sun Microsystems. Gosling and others
on his team set out to find a language that would catch the
next wave of computing. Catch it they did, as the language
is commonly used in thousands of applications in our daily
computing lives. These include Internet chat rooms; virtual
games such as checkers, chess and cards; and other graphi-
cal Web applications.

Adults and Their Toys

Not everything created for American enterprise has to be utilitarian. Some things have been created just for fun. Toys exemplify an industry built on one of the most influential groups in consumer spending—children. Behind most toys is an interesting story. As trivial as their ideas may seem, it's easy to argue that they're actually the work of genius when you contemplate the longevity they have enjoyed in the lives of children. Here are some adults and the toys they created.[1]

1. MORRIS MICHTOM—THE TEDDY BEAR

Theodore Roosevelt was an outdoorsman and a hunter, but he also loved animals. On one occasion, he was hunting with some of his aides and a group of reporters. For several days the newspapers reported that the president had failed to shoot any game and depicted this in a political cartoon. Finally, Roosevelt's aides found a bear, which they cornered and presented to him as a trophy. However, Roosevelt felt compassion for the bear and refused to shoot it. A Brooklyn storeowner, Morris Michtom, saw the drawing of Roosevelt

[1] Information gathered from www.historychannel.com/exhibits/toys.

and the bear cub and was inspired to create a new toy. He created a little stuffed bear cub and put it in his shop window with a sign that read "Teddy's bear." The toys were an immediate success, and Michtom founded the Ideal Novelty and Toy Co., which still exists today.

2. FRED MORRISON—THE FRISBEE

Even the least athletic of teenagers enjoys throwing Frisbees, but few know anything about the toy's history and less still about how it flies. The name comes from the Frisbie Pie Company, which made pie plates. In the late 1800s students at Yale University discovered that the pie plates had unusual aerodynamic characteristics; that is, they could be sent into a flying spin fairly easily. The rest is history! Part-time inventor Fred Morrison experimented with the saucers and made some models by pressing plastic into the disc shape. Eventually he sold his design to Wham-O Toy Company, which marketed the disc so successfully that the toy is known by the masses as the Frisbee.

3. ELLIOT AND RUTH HANDLER—THE BARBIE DOLL

First introduced at the American International Toy Fair in New York in 1959, Barbie was the product of Elliot Handler and his wife, Ruth, cofounders of Mattel, Inc. The doll was named after their daughter, Barbie. Ken, who later came on to the scene, also has significance, as he represented the couple's son. The Barbie doll wasn't a smash hit right out of the starting gate. But almost fifty years later the Barbie doll is one of the most successful and enduring toys on the market.

4. CHARLES DARROW—MONOPOLY

Once an engineer from Germantown, Pennsylvania, Darrow was unemployed during the Great Depression. He ventured into creating a game printed on an oilcloth and created it right on his kitchen table. His proximity to the New Jersey shore fueled his curiosity and led him to include geographical landmarks in a game about buying and selling properties in a pretend world. He used street and property names in Atlantic City in a game of chance and skill and in 1934 presented the game idea to Parker Brothers. His idea was criticized for having too many design errors and was rejected. Critics felt it was downright complicated and slow. Faced with these obstacles, Darrow ventured out on his own to sell the game to other interested parties. After seeing that interest in the game had been aroused, Parker Brothers changed its mind and bought the rights to Monopoly for an undisclosed sum.

5. DONALD DUNCAN—THE YO-YO

Duncan was an entrepreneur who had already had success with some off-the-beaten path innovations like the parking meter, movie screen, and the Eskimo pie. In 1928 Duncan was in Los Angeles and spotted a young man named Pedro Flores demonstrating his yo-yo. Duncan liked the toy, so much so that he bought Flores's company and hired hundreds of "Yo-Yo Men" to travel the country demonstrating tricks, like "walking the dog" and "around the world." This created demand for the toy, and a new market was born. It is believed that the yo-yo was actually used thousands of years earlier by Greeks. It has lasted the test of time and is still found everywhere around the globe.

6. EDWIN BINNEY AND C. HAROLD SMITH—THE CRAYON

At the turn of the twentieth century, Binney & Smith, a chemical company, produced slate pencils and classroom chalk. Edwin Binney and C. Harold Smith were cousins and the namesake of the chemical company. They had developed a new wax crayon to mark crates and boxes in their factory. This was a neater and more affordable alternative to similar products that had been coming in from Europe. They developed the crayons to be nontoxic and easy to mass-produce. The crayon has become a mainstay in American culture.

7. ALFRED MOSHER BUTTS AND JAMES BRUNOT—SCRABBLE

In the early 1930s an unemployed architect got creative. He wanted to cross-pollinate board games with anagrams and word puzzles. After studying the front page of the *New York Times*, he calculated the frequency of certain letters to limit the ease of a word game. More frequent letters received a lower point value in his newfound game. After striking out in selling the game idea, Butts sold his idea to Connecticut entrepreneur James Brunot, who named it "Scrabble"—meaning to grapple frantically for something. Brunot and his wife made the games in their home and managed to get enough orders for the project to take off. Eventually he sold the game to a major manufacturer.

8. RICHARD JAMES—THE SLINKY

James was a World War II naval engineer who studied springs to find a means of easing the shipboard motion of naval vessels. As luck would have it, James discovered that a torsion spring can actually walk, given the right input of motion. It was James's wife who gave it the name "Slinky." Thus began the amazing toy that found its way into the homes of the masses.

9. ARTHUR MELIN AND RICHARD KNERR—THE HULA HOOP

These two innovators got the idea from a friend who saw schoolchildren in Australia slinging bamboo hoops in a harmonic motion around their waste. Like the yo-yo, the Hula Hoop is thought to have originated in ancient times. Some cite its origination as early as 1000 B.C. in Egypt. If anything stands the test of time, it may well be the Hula Hoop. The first year it was introduced, fifteen million of them were produced.

10. ELEANOR ABBOTT—CANDY LAND

Abbot had been struck with polio. While recovering in her California home, she designed games for children who had been struck with the dreaded disease. Candy Land was kid-friendly, with ample reference to yummy places like Peppermint Stick Forest and Gum Drop Mountain. The concept stuck and Milton Bradley bought the idea. Candy Land has also stood the test of time for children of all generations as a game with a sweet subject that doesn't give you cavities.

Show 'Em the Factory

I t used to be a sales tactic in the age of smokestacks and manufacturing lines. Bringing in potential customers and showing them how your products are made has always been intriguing to both industrial and consumer customers alike. Today, there still are many manufacturers that welcome the public to come in and see how their cola, candy, or recreational vehicles are made. If you ever want to consult one of the finest directories that will tell you which companies offer factory tours, then get to a bookstore and pick up *Watch It Made in the USA* by Karen Axelrod and Bruce Brumberg (2002). It is a treasure chest of information about factory tours that is well written and researched and a great way to enhance a family vacation. Here are ten firms with factory floors worth visiting.[1]

1. THE JELLY BEAN CANDY COMPANY

The Fairfield, California, company prides itself on its factory tours. The company makes some 14 billion jelly beans each

[1] Information gathered from *Watch It Made in the USA*, by Karen Axelrod and Bruce Brumberg (New York: Avalon Travel Publishing, 2002).

year. Spread these 14 billion out among 400 different flavors, and you're talking some serious permutations for operations managers at the Jelly Bean Candy Company. Visitors can tour the facility and watch something most have never seen before—how jelly beans are made. It's rumored that all visitors receive a three-ounce bag of jelly beans as a sampler after the tour.

2.   THE JOHN DEERE COMPANY

Drive through the heartland of America and our "amber waves of grain," and you just might see a green machine busy at work in a spacious, crop-filled field. John Deere tractors and farm equipment are made deep in the heart of Moline, Illinois. When you stop in Moline, this tour is simply the thing to do. Visitors are able to witness the full-fledged assembly of the green equipment with yellow lettering and ornamentation. Right before your eyes, you can see the equipment come to life on the assembly line and go off to aid agricultural production throughout the world.

3.   THE CAPE COD POTATO CHIP COMPANY

Hundreds of thousands visit Cape Cod, in the town of Hyannis, Massachusetts, each year, including the Kennedy family, who has summered for generations at their Hyannis home. Amid its natural beaches, lobster boils, and nautical settings is a small industrial production line churning out potato chips. The factory is open to the public and offers a grand tour of what are some of the finest, all-natural kettle-cooked potato chips. You'll learn not only how potato chips are made, but when you receive your free sample bag at the end of the tour, you'll also learn that Cape Cod makes a darn good potato chip.

4.   PURINA FARMS

Welcome to Gray Summit, Missouri—home to Purina Farms. Here you'll find a complex that encompasses the landscape of pets and pet food of all types. Not only can visitors see the pet food being made, but they can also take side trips on the compound to a petting zoo and the oldest and largest animal nutrition center of its kind. Purina Farms also presents a variety of animal shows, including dog training shows, dog swimming demonstrations, and cow milking demonstrations. The pet-centric site may be as animal-friendly as one could ask for.

5. THE BUCK KNIVES CORPORATION

If you're a "knife person," then you just may have found a hot spot for your dream vacation in El Cajon, California. The Buck Knives Corporation has been forging quality pocket-knives for the better half of the last century. Their knives are the envy of hunters, fishermen, woodsmen, and modern-day adult Tom Sawyers everywhere. Visitors can see the knives made in full assembly from unfinished steel to the final test of a new product.

6. HUSH PUPPY SHOES

Everybody knows them. Look for a shoebox with a sad little basset hound on the box, and you've found some Hush Puppy shoes. The Wolverine World Wide Shoe Company, which makes Hush Puppies, is located in Rockford, Michigan, and is the manufacturing site of the quintessential suede shoe of our homeland. Introduced in 1957, these shoes are still in production, and visitors can see them made by walking right onto the factory floor.

7. THE AIRSTREAM CORPORATION

If you ever go to Jackson Center, Ohio, you'll want to visit the manufacturing mecca of the Airstream Corporation—maker of one of the most prestigious recreational vehicles in America. You've seen them. They're the sleek trailers being pulled behind vacationers round the world. They bear a semblance to an overlarge silver bullet being towed behind a vehicle. The vehicles are actually constructed of high-grade aluminum. They're an invention of Wally Byam, who built his own trailer back in the early 1930s when his wife wouldn't go camping without her kitchen. His design imitated aircraft with a riveted shell that was aerodynamically smooth. Today Byam's creations dot the highways and byways the world over.

8. THE AMERICAN WHISTLE COMPANY

If you stay in Ohio, you can divert to Columbus and visit another manufacturer you likely have never heard of before: the Great American Whistle Company. The chrome-plated whistles you see being blown by referees, policemen, and drill sergeants throughout the world just may have been manufactured at this site. Visitors to the plant learn about whistle technology. You'll learn just how that little ball is put into a whistle, how whistles sound, and why American whistles are a cut above any old whistle. Visitors receive a chrome-finish whistle as a token for their visit. The tour is ideal for the curious and for those who want to know the story behind an ordinary object we see and hear regularly.

9. TOM'S OF MAINE

They're simple products with a simple name. The company's location is upscale and sophisticated Kennebunk-port, Maine, the summer home of former president George H. W. Bush. Tom's of Maine manufactures all-natural hygiene products from toothpaste to mouthwash and deodorant. The company is the work of Tom and Kate Chappell, who moved to Maine for a simpler life. Visitors watch happy production workers in a low-stress production environment. Visitors to the company's plant will see the interesting operation that the Chappells have built in a converted railroad station. They'll also walk away with a product fresh off the production line.

10. POMPEIAN OLIVE OIL

Not all olive oil is made in Spain or Italy. Baltimore, Maryland, is the manufacturing site for Pompeian Olive Oil and

Red Wine Vinegar. Visitors to the plant will gain a wealth of information about a product that is increasing in popularity as a healthy form of fat in our diet and an age-old staple of epicureans. The tours are tailored to the audience and allow the visitor to sample the aroma, taste, and technology behind olive oil and red wine vinegar—made in America.

Doing Business with Uncle Sam

B usiness isn't just about serving for-profit customers. There's also a large chunk of the economy that feeds off the U.S. federal government. Government defense contracting is somewhat of a cyclical business in that contractors' revenues are often dependent upon government contracts that change over time. There are, however, a few contractors that always seem to find their way into the top ten list. Here are some government contractors that have been in the top ten and will likely be at or near the top ten for years to come.

1. THE LOCKHEED MARTIN COMPANY

The company is a result of a merger between the Lockheed Corporation and the Martin-Marietta Corporation. A mainstay in the aerospace industry, Lockheed Martin is now such a huge conglomerate that it probably does a little bit of just about everything when it comes to making equipment and systems for the U.S. government and many other governments around the globe. In 2002 the company was awarded some $17 billion in government contracts. It has garnered the number one spot on the list of U.S. defense contractors on more than one occasion and will likely hold that spot more than once again.

2. THE BOEING CORPORATION

You know the company from the old days of hearing about the Boeing 747. Those were the days when flying in a 747 was all the rage. The Seattle-based company is in the news from time to time for its big defense contract awards as well as its big commercial contract awards. Or you may hear about the company because its union called a strike. Recently, though, the company moved its headquarters to Chicago, Illinois, from its long-standing Seattle base and left poor old Starbucks Coffee all by itself in the Northwestern city. In 2002 Boeing had nearly $17 billion in defense contracts and, like Lockheed Martin, you'll find it on the top-ten list of defense contractors in any given year. The big guys just never go away.

3. NORTHROP GRUMMAN CORPORATION

The company that built much of the equipment and vehicles used in the Apollo space program also made navy fighter jets and owns a controlling interest in Newport News Shipbuilding, which is the nuclear engineering mecca of the world. The company racked up some $8.7 billion in government contracts through its various divisions and subsidiaries and frequently finds its way into the top ten list of defense contractors.

4. RAYTHEON CORPORATION

The Massachussetts-based company has been a bastion of defense electronics and is a worldwide leader in navigational equipment. Like its defense contractor counterparts, Raytheon has a full regiment of subsidiary companies, including Raytheon Aerospace Holdings, Raytheon Training, Raytheon Service, and several global subsidiaries in the U.K. and Canada. It culled some $7 billion in defense contracts in the early part of the new millennium and has had a venerable presence in service to the defense of our nation. Sadly, Raytheon lost several of its employees on one of the aircraft that crashed in the events of 9/11/01.

5. GENERAL DYNAMICS CORPORATION

This big player didn't make its money just in things that fly, but also in things that float; that is, things that float on the water and under it. Yes, General Dynamics has built a large share of the U.S. Navy's submarines. So many that Groton, Connecticut, is one of the navy's nuclear submarine bases, because it's close to where General Dynamics builds its submarines. The company also owns the Bath Iron Works shipbuilding in Bath, Maine, and NASSCO Holdings, another shipbuilding giant, on the West Coast. The company does about $6 billion in defense contracting and is almost always in the top ten or twenty on the defense contractor list.

6. UNITED TECHNOLOGIES CORPORATION

This company is a multiconglomerate made up of technology companies, including some recognizable names such as Carrier Corporation, the air conditioning people in Syracuse, New York, and the Pratt-Whitney subsidiary, which makes gas turbine engines and other engineering technology. Based in the Northeast near Hartford, Connecticut, United Technologies did about $3.6 billion in defense contracting in the early part of the new millennium.

7. SCIENCE APPLICATIONS INTERNATIONAL CORPORATION (SAIC)

Here's one you probably never heard of. SAIC is a silent giant in the defense contracting ranks, based in San Diego, California, with many offices scattered throughout the United States. It seems to have a big piece of the pie when it comes to defense dollars. It owns a few subsidiary companies that do engineering design and information technology consulting and design, among other technical services. The company pulled in about 2 billion defense dollars in 2002.

8. TRW INCORPORATED

TRW has also been a stronghold in the defense contracting arena. The company has several large subsidiaries and possesses a particular strength in defense electronics and information technology. The company has just under $2 billion from its defense contracts and is often in the top twenty, if not top ten, on the list of defense contractors.

9. HEALTH NET, INC.

Here's another company you may not know on the surface. It, too, is a big defense contractor. Health Net, Inc., is one of the nation's largest publicly traded managed health-care companies. The company's HMO, insured PPO, and government contract subsidiaries provide health benefits to approximately 5.3 million individuals in fifteen states through group, individual, Medicare, Medicaid, and TRICARE programs. These include the U.S. military members and retirees who receive many medical services through them. The very fact that the company is one of the top defense contractors proves that it's not just airplanes, submarines, and rockets that are expensive—our health and proper care are too. The company drew in about 1.6 billion defense dollars in 2002.

10. GENERAL ELECTRIC

The company has been a part of the landscape of U.S. defense for decades and continues to be so. Based in Fairfield, Connecticut, this industrial giant makes aircraft engines that go into a multitude of U.S. Navy fighter jets. It also produces motors, electronics, plastics, nuclear services, and a wide array of products that usually put it at or near the top ten list of defense contractors. The firm did about $1.6 billion with the U.S. Department of Defense in 2002 and is a household name as well as a major defense contractor.

From the Laboratory

Trial and error has driven much advancement in capitalism over the centuries. Things are tried. If they work, they're expanded upon, and if they don't, they're killed. This process has certainly been the force behind research and development for technology-savvy companies. Some companies do their own R&D, but many contract such services out with research grants to public and private universities throughout the nation. If you look at the brainpower of a university to create patents, you'll find a fairly diverse mixture of patent-creating schools of higher education. Here are some of the leading colleges and universities and the number of patents they were granted in the year 2002.[1]

1. UNIVERSITY OF CALIFORNIA

With a grand total of 431 patents, this university system took the lead in 2002 and is at the top of universities that produce patents. This is the largest state in the union with a very large university system. Credit its size, or credit its outstanding ability to create patents, but it comes in first.

[1] Information gathered from www.uspto.gov.

2. MASSACHUSETTS INSTITUTE OF TECHNOLOGY

With 135 patents in 2002, the mecca of science and technology is notorious for its scientific prowess. Incidentally, the school that had the highest number of patents had one of the highest rates of suicide in the same year. In any event the long-standing and well-deserved reputation of MIT as a powerhouse for the best and brightest in engineering and science is evident with a top slot in the number of patents churned out. The MIT community is also home to a large number of Nobel Prize winners.

3. CALIFORNIA INSTITUTE OF TECHNOLOGY

With 109 patents, the Pasadena, California–based university is right up there. It's the home of the Jet Propulsion Laboratory and many well-known bastions of science and technology. Some heavy-hitting aerospace companies in the Los Angeles area surround the school's location, and CIT also has access to undergraduates from other leading patent-generating universities throughout the state.

4. STANFORD UNIVERSITY

With 104 patents, Stanford is in good company. We've hardly left California in ferreting out the top patent generators. Stanford isn't far from the famed Silicon Valley. This monumental positioning near the geographic center of computer technology puts the university in a natural position to provide patented products to this as well as many other industries.

5. UNIVERSITY OF TEXAS

With 93 patents, this university makes George W. Bush proud. Centered in the state's capital of Austin, the University of Texas is another state university in a very large state. As such, it has a bigger talent pool to draw from, and, well, it has turned whatever advantages it may have into a patent-developing university. Go Longhorns! (Author claims no affiliation.)

6. JOHNS HOPKINS UNIVERSITY

With 81 patents, the Maryland-based university isn't just known for lacrosse. Johns Hopkins has a fine reputation in academics, medicine, and sports. Whatever it does, it does it quite well, because next to MIT, Johns Hopkins seems to lead the eastern states with the number of patents acquired by a university—at least in the year 2002, that is.

7. UNIVERSITY OF WISCONSIN

And now for something completely different. With 81 patents, the University of Wisconsin has proved that America's Dairyland has a state university system that's not only innovative, but also creative, enterprising, and fired with a high level of intellect. So much so that it is right up there in its contribution to the world with patents produced.

8. STATE UNIVERSITY OF NEW YORK

"If you can make it there, you'll make it anywhere"—or is that just the *city* of New York that Sinatra sings about? The state university system rang in some 55 patents in 2002. Like many of the others, it's a huge state university system, with some wonders of the world to draw from. It seems to use its resources well, as it is a leading patent producer.

9. PENNSYLVANIA STATE UNIVERSITY

If Johns Hopkins isn't just lacrosse, Penn State isn't just football. The university was responsible for 50 patents in 2002. Drive into Pennsylvania and you'll see a big sign that says "America Starts Here." You'll also see that message on the state's Web site and on nearly every license plate issued in the state. Add to all of this a top patent-producing university, and, whew, you have some impressive credentials in the state of Pennsylvania. Next time you drive through the state, you may whisper to yourself, "American Patents Start Here Too."

10. **MICHIGAN STATE UNIVERSITY**

With 49 patents in 2002, Michigan State just missed the
mark and wound up behind Penn State in this ranking. Like
the Nittany Lions, it isn't just about football either. It is a top
patent producer in a state where it contends with the University of Michigan for so much, but in this particular year and
in this particular department—the Spartans beat 'em!

Getting It There

Transportation hasn't just moved people; it has also moved products. Today we want everything immediately, and if it hadn't been for a few notable heroes of fast package delivery, we wouldn't have the convenience of door-to-door delivery that we have today. Here are a few milestones that have made "getting it there" something of a magical occurrence in today's instant-coffee mind-set.[1]

1. THE FOUNDING OF WELLS FARGO (1852)

You've seen them in the movies, and you've heard the tall tales and the lore of the stagecoach. Founded by Henry Wells and William G. Fargo in 1852, Wells Fargo was not the only private carrier of its day, but it blazed a new trail in moving goods from the new frontier West to other destinations throughout the new land.

2. THE FOUNDING OF THE PONY EXPRESS (1860)

The service is heavy on legend and tradition, but it wasn't as prosperous as you might have thought. The need for its ser-

[1] Information gathered from www.treas.gov/offices/domestic-finance/usps/docs/parcel_history_final.doc.

vice was there, but the Pony Express wasn't truly profitable. It charged a hefty $1.00 for a half-ounce letter, which would equate to about $23 in today's pocket. The service just wasn't on the list of affordable things for people of its day. However, the Pony Express did make it possible for goods to be delivered for those who could afford it. The company was sold to Wells Fargo in 1866.

3. THE COMPLETION OF THE TRANSCONTINENTAL RAILROAD (1869)

In 1869 the Central and the Union Pacific Railroads were joined at Promontory Summit, Utah. Goods could now be moved by way of a mechanically powered mode of transportation. Such technological introduction transformed the movement of packaged freight. Wells Fargo was still in swing and competed with the U.S. Postal Service when the railroad service came around. The railroad's freight conveyance gave way to a new method of moving packaged goods.

4. THE FORMATION OF UPS GROUND SERVICE (1907)

In 1907 Jim Casey and Claude Ryan, two teens from Seattle, began the American Message Company. The company delivered packages and ran errands on foot and by bicycle, with only a few deliveries made by motorcar. Their efforts were the beginning of the courier concept of package delivery. The company steadily grew to encompass more than Seattle and was renamed United Parcel Service in 1930.

5. PARCEL POST (1913)

In 1913 parcel post was a limited package delivery service provided by the U.S. Post Office. Before this time, merchants brought their goods to the nearest transportation center for a private delivery service to ship them out. A strange and amusing abuse of the Parcel Post system occurred when someone shipped an entire bank building, one brick at a time.

6. THE FORMATION OF THE RAILWAY EXPRESS AGENCY (REA) (1929)

Wells Fargo and six other express companies bargained for the creation of the Railway Express Agency in 1929. Though it's no longer in existence, it was in business for over fifty-six years. Similar to the identifiable trucks of today's UPS and FedEx, the REA's green trucks and rail cars were the trademark for many expecting a package delivery.

7. THE ESTABLISHMENT OF THE INTERSTATE HIGHWAY SYSTEM (1956)

This is something we all have gratitude for, as it allows us to travel freely and quickly by land to many different places. What it did for package delivery was to help build a transcontinental network of superhighways. The Interstate Highway System gave way to the enactment of airline deregulation in 1978, interstate trucking deregulation in 1980, and intrastate trucking deregulation in 1994, which contributed to the significant shift to truck and air transport, especially during the latter part of this period, and marked the growth of the modern package delivery industry.

8. THE FOUNDING OF UPS AIR OPERATIONS (1953)

In 1929 United Parcel Service (UPS) opened United Air Express. This air package delivery arm offered air express delivery to West Coast cities. UPS had previously tried air travel but had difficulty competing in this arena. Due to the stock market crash, United Air Express had to shut down operations after only eight months of existence. It wasn't until 1953 that UPS resumed air service, offering two-day service to major cities on the East and West Coasts with packages being carried in the belly of regularly scheduled airlines.

9. THE FORMATION OF FEDERAL EXPRESS

What would we do without Federal Express? Federal Express began its operations on April 17, 1973, with the launch of fourteen small aircraft from Memphis International Airport. Fred Smith had actually written a paper on the concept of a focused hub where shipments would be consolidated, sorted, and redistributed to their destination. The idea for his sort-and-distribute concept for package delivery came about somewhat by accident. Smith was working on obtaining a contract with the Federal Reserve Bank, and although the proposal was denied, he believed the name was appropriate for express envelope and small package delivery.

10. THE EVOLUTION OF E-COMMERCE

Today's Internet seems light-years away from the antiquated methods of the dusty trails traveled by Wells Fargo. Investments and improvements in information technology have enabled package carriers to provide customers with tracking information for packages as they move from origin to destination. Later advances combine logistics with traditional package delivery in managing finance and inventory accounting for a full supply-chain management solution. In addition, software, books, music, and documents can now be transported electronically right onto a desktop computer. By some estimates, packaged goods shipped by air and ground are valued between 8.6 percent and 14.3 percent of the nation's Gross Domestic Product. Whew! Talk about progress!

Work from Home and Make a Gazillion Dollars

I n the past, a home-based business was viewed as a side business operated primarily as a hobby or as a source of secondary income. The home-based contribution to the U.S. economy is about 5 percent of the total contribution of all small employer firms with fewer than five hundred employees. The home-based business sector is growing in importance, driven by the revolution in information technology. It also offers opportunities for entrepreneurs and at-home professionals in every demographic and ethnic group. But the home-based business has been misunderstood.

Perhaps the reason for this misunderstanding is that not much information is available about home-based businesses. What does exist, however, is ample propaganda that sells and promises success and the dream of being able to operate businesses out of one's home. The U.S. Small Business Administration did a study in 1997 and found some information that most people never knew or understood about home-based businesses.[1]

[1] Information gathered from www.ftc.gov and www.sba.gov.

1. SEEK COMMUNITY

Home-based does not necessarily mean a one-person show. About 19 percent of home-based firms have employees.

2. NOT NECESSARILY BIG-BUCK OPERATIONS

Big-buck revenues do not characterize home-based businesses, on average. In 1997 the average receipt of all home-based firms was in the $40,000 range, with some variance by demographic group. Beginning at $50,000, an increasingly greater percentage of firms are likely to be non–home-based.

3. CLERICAL IS KING

There's much success in mundane business services such as clerical services or paperwork. Of the three general business uses of the home—for clerical work, for production work, and for telecommuting—the most money by far is made by firms that use the home for clerical work. Firms owned by men were more likely to use the home for clerical tasks; firms owned by women were more likely to use the home to produce goods or services on the premises.

4. SHOESTRING IS IN

The home-based business can be started on a shoestring. In 1997, 40 to 44 percent of all home-based businesses required less than $5,000 for startup. Another 25 percent or so needed $5,000 to $25,000. By contrast, a quarter of non–home-based firms needed more than $25,000 to start.

5. STAY AT HOME

Moving the business up and out to succeed is not always necessary. Home-based firms tend to remain in the home—fewer than 5 percent eventually move out of the home. There is some evidence that capital constraints prevent more firms from expanding. Some industries, such as construction, transportation, communications, and utilities, show about the same profit whether operated in the home or outside of the home. In these cases, the home is generally used for clerical work.

6. HOURS ARE DOWN

Home-based-business owners don't put in as many hours as their counterparts—owners work on average twenty-six to thirty-five hours per week in their firms. By contrast, owners of non-home-based businesses work an average of thirty-five to forty-three hours per week.

7. SURVIVAL IS BRIGHT

The survival outlook of a home-based business is bright. Over half of all home-based businesses survive five years. Firms that close do so primarily from lack of cash or access to a business loan. When the Small Business Administration studied these businesses in the early 1990s, about 85 percent of firms with paid employees survived, compared with 51 percent of those that had no paid employees.

8. AUTOMATE

Business success strategies of using credit cards and Web sites are the smart way to go. These two areas expedite a company's payment and order-taking ability and help shape an Internet strategy. As Internet commerce becomes more sophisticated, more capital will be required for at-home businesses to develop and maintain profitable Web-based companies.

9. WHERE TO LOCATE

Location matters little. The use of technology allows home-based businesses to work in teams without the need for daily face-to-face interaction. This allows a firm to expand beyond the physical confines of a residence while expanding sales.

10. THE INDIVIDUAL MARKET

Home-based businesses sell to individuals—in fact, 60 percent of home-based businesses sell primarily to individuals.

Roughly 10 percent of customers are local, state, and federal government agencies. Slightly more firms owned by African Americans sell to the government than the other demographic groups, according to the Small Business Administration. Firms owned by non-minority males showed the highest business-to-business sales, at 43 percent.

Kids' Play

It sounds juvenile to learn about the serious side of kids' cereals, but don't let the bright colors and snappy characters fool you. Kids' cereals are big business—big, *serious* business. A cadre of recognizable cartoon characters who provide brand identification to influence consumers to purchase certain cereals over others has marked the twentieth century at the morning breakfast table. Here are some of the most notable cartoon characters on the cereal box.[1]

1. THE TRIX RABBIT

The Trix rabbit was first created in 1959 with the expression "Trix are for kids, not for silly rabbits." One might argue that the cereal indeed looks like rabbit food, with tiny round pellets that are "raspberry red, lemon yellow, and orange orange."

2. CAP'N CRUNCH

Who doesn't have a special place in their heart for the salty sea captain? Cap'n Crunch was created by the Quaker Oats

[1] Information gathered from www.lavasurfer.com/cereal-guide.html.

Company in 1963. He lives on Crunch Island and sails the S.S. *Guppy* with his first mate, Seadog. Kids around the nation have followed his adventures by reading the back of the box and saving box tops to get promotional goodies from Cap'n Crunch, his crew, and all their associated friends.

3. TONY THE TIGER

Unless you lived your entire childhood under a rock, you know that Tony is the zealous tiger who claims that his flakes are "Grrrrrreat!" Created sometime around 1951 by Kellogg's, Tony has lasted the test of time and remains on cereal boxes in most any store around the world.

4. THE FRUIT LOOP TOUCAN

Toucan Sam is his name, and he is a true icon of identity when it comes to Fruit Loops. Kellogg's has kept him on the box since about 1963. In that time, you may have noticed some changes to his beak, his colors, and the spin on the products—marshmallow Fruit Loops and, more recently, low-sugar Fruit Loops.

5. THE QUAKER MAN

In 1877 Quaker Oats was the first company to trademark a character on its cereals. That Quaker figure, with his wide-brimmed hat and slight grin, has come to be known the world over—mostly as a sign of its oatmeal products, though the company makes a myriad of other, non-cereal products as well. Little did Quaker Oats know that it would create a means of marketing breakfast cereal that will probably endure forever.

6. THE CREAM OF WHEAT CHEF

Well, he has a name: Rastus, the Cream of Wheat chef, was created around 1890 by Emery Mapes, who was part owner of the Diamond Milling Company in North Dakota. The image of Rastus that we see today, however, was created in the 1920s. The story goes that the model was a Chicago waiter who was paid five dollars to pose in the white chef's hat and jacket. He's African American, always smiling, and always happy, serving up the hot cereal that has found its way into the cereal's advertising and age-old brand image.

7. THE LUCKY CHARMS LEPRECHAUN

Okay, how do they taste? If you said "magically delicious," you are right on and in the know when it comes to kids' breakfast cereals. The leprechaun character came about in 1964, just about the time when most other kids' cereals launched some of their most enduring characters who found their way on the box and stayed there. The oat cereal was originally complemented with marshmallow bits in the shapes of pink hearts, orange stars, yellow moons, and green clovers. The company continues to dabble with various shapes for its "marbits," as those at General Mills call them.

8. THE CALIFORNIA RAISINS

Even Raisin Bran can be brought to life by an ad agency's creativity. In fact, Post's potentially lackluster cereal was very much brought to life and into the limelight when the California Raisins were created by Foote, Cone, and Belding and animated by Claymation artist Bill Vinton. Vinton's production company came up with a commercial where the California Raisins sang "Heard It Through the Grapevine." Unlike many of the traditional cereal characters, these wrinkled singing fruits weren't created until the late 1980s. They even had their own television series from September 1989 until September 1990!

9. SUGAR BEAR

Post Sugar Crisp and follow-on brands were characterized by this friendly, sweet honey bear in the ribbed-neck turtleneck sweater. He was introduced in the early 1960s along with many other famous cereal characters and briefly had a television series of his own on CBS. With a voice that sounded something like Dean Martin (but was actually voiced by Gerry Matthews), Sugar Bear would risk his hide to get his Sugar Crisp cereal, and perhaps programmed the minds of kids in their living rooms in front of the newfound boob tube during the 1960s to do the same. In today's health-conscious world, however, the cereal has been renamed and is now called "Golden Crisp."

10. SNAP, CRACKLE, AND POP

Since 1933 Rice Krispies have been personified with these three onomatopoeic characters who, like their competitors, josh and jeer with each other and represent the selling point of the Rice Krispies cereal, which does exactly what the names say—snap, crackle, and pop. These little gnomes were created well ahead of some of the more famous cereal characters, and each wears his own signature hat. Snap wears a baker's hat, Crackle has a red-and-white-striped stocking cap, and Pop is topped with a military hat. Snap started it all by being introduced in 1933. Crackle and Pop came along in 1941. All three are immortal, and you can find them on a box of Rice Krispies even today.

Creating a Monopoly

I t's difficult to discuss American business without mentioning the legacy of Monopoly. The game has been enjoyed
by many generations and has a pure business and enterprise
flavor to it. The board game of property acquisition, control,
and chance is one that entertains and reflects of our capitalist economy. When a game can last for so long and be re-
created in so many different forms and formats, a closer look
is due its lesser-known particularities. Here are ten little tidbits of information you may not have known about the game.[1]

1. **HIGH ODDS**

A 1996 issue of *Scientific American* magazine featured an
article that gave the probabilities of landing on some of the
squares of Monopoly. For example, visiting jail was one of
the most probable, with a 3.944 percent probability.

2. **SHOW US THE MONEY**

It is rumored that more money is printed each year to ac-
company the production of this game than is printed as U.S.

[1] Information gathered from www.monopoly.com and www.tkcs-
collins.com/truman/monopoly/monopoly.shtml.

currency by the Department of the Treasury. The Monopoly .com Web site allows you to print your own money for free!

3. DARROW THE DEVELOPER

The game was developed by Charles B. Darrow, who invented the game while he was unemployed in or about 1933. He was inspired by another game called The Landlord. He gleaned the game's property titles from his visits to Atlantic City, New Jersey. Parker Brothers rejected his original idea, because it had some fifty-two errors in it. Darrow later became a millionaire, and the game has become one of the best sellers for Hasbro, which now owns the game's rights.

4. ODD PRINTING

Early versions of the game had a representation of its founder, Charles B. Darrow, printed on the jail square. Marvin Gardens was once twenty-two dollars rent, but was later changed to twenty-four dollars. Early versions had no pictures printed on the cards. Early property cards were blank on the back.

5. THE RAILROADS

Three of the four railroads in the game are names of actual railroads that carried wealthy vacationers to Atlantic City at the time. The Short Line is the fourth and was actually the name of a bus service that carried freight and had a depot in the environs of Atlantic City.

6. MONOPOLY ON THE GO

For about thirty dollars you can play Monopoly on your pocket PC. Wherever you are, you can use your stylus to play the game of chance and property ownership.

7. THE CHAMPIONS

The world Monopoly championship is held each year and has gained much enthusiasm in Asian countries. It was won by someone from Hong Kong in 1996, and in 2000 the championship was held in Japan. The 2003 championship was played aboard a train ride from Chicago to the founding town of Atlantic City.

8. MULTIPLE AVENUES

Monopoly is no longer just a board game. There's Monopoly Junior, Pokemon Monopoly, Monopoly Card Game, Disney Monopoly, Monopoly for Game Boy Games, and a myriad of other places that the owner has sold its license to in order to milk every nickel of profit the world-famous Monopoly brand name can conjure up.

9. MONOPOLY SCANDAL

The game faced some controversy in 1974 when a university professor badmouthed the game's risk and exploitation of monopolies and property acquisitions. The professor had invented a game called Anti-Monopoly, a game in which players could break up big business monopolies, which landed him in a lawsuit. He lost his case and was forced to bury thousands of sets of the game in a Minnesota garbage dump. But after winning two appeals to the U.S. Supreme Court, the Anti-Monopoly game was reintroduced in 1984.

10. MONOPOLY THE OFFICIAL WEB SITE

The home for Monopoly-crazed fanatics. This site is chock-full of interesting facts and information such as: the longest Monopoly game was about 99 hours; Monopoly is published in 26 languages in 80 different countries and boasts some 500 million players around the globe; a standard set of Monopoly includes $15,140 in play money; in the French version of the game "Boardwalk" is called "Rue de la Paix."

The Good Guys

W ho says that the only goal of a corporation is to turn a profit for its shareholders? Social responsibility is a watchword for many business leaders. Giving back to the community through their employees and their volunteerism is what these ten companies do quite well.[1]

1. AT&T

With the AT&T CARES program, AT&T employees can receive one day of paid leave each year for community service activities. The company reports that 65 percent of its employees volunteered in their communities in 2001, and since the program's inception in 1996, employees have contributed over four million hours to such activities. The company also provides an intranet site where employees can coordinate community service projects and recruit other employee volunteers. In addition, employees and retirees are encouraged to participate in special twice-yearly volunteer team initiatives.

[1] Information gathered from www.usafreedomcorps.gov/content/about_usafc/newsroom/announcements_dynamic.asp?ID=37.

2. **COMCAST CABLE COMMUNICATIONS, INC.**

On its annual "Comcast Cares Day," Comcast employees are encouraged to volunteer in their local communities. In 2003 Comcast created an hour-long prime-time national broadcast that highlighted and encouraged volunteerism. They also conducted a national public service announcement campaign.

3. **FEDERAL EXPRESS CORPORATION**

FedEx contributes valuable resources to communities through volunteerism, corporate donations, complimentary shipping, and alliances with major charities. The company sponsors a program called SAFE KIDS Walk This Way, which aims to prevent accidental childhood injuries—the number one killer of children ages fourteen and under. FedEx is also a major supporter of the ORBIS (a program for prevention and treatment of blindness) and United Way programs.

4. **MARRIOTT INTERNATIONAL, INC.**

Marriott's "Spirit to Serve Our Communities" program encourages its employees to get involved in community service through volunteering and other efforts. Thousands of Marriott employees volunteer on the company's "global day of giving" each May; they also participate throughout the year in other company-sponsored programs and local initiatives.

5. **OXYGEN MEDIA**

Oxygen Media has always placed a great deal of importance on advocacy and volunteerism on behalf of women and issues that are important to them. Each year the company's employees receive a half day of paid leave for volunteerism and service. In 2001 the company launched its "Choose to Lead" program to promote leadership opportunities for women, especially in public offices. The program won an award for Public, Community Relations, and Event Marketing from the Cable and Telecommunications Association for Marketing.

6. HOME DEPOT

Home Depot sets an annual goal for volunteer hours and challenges its employees to meet that goal. The company is involved in disaster assistance programs, Habitat for Humanity, programs for at-risk youths, job programs for Olympic athletes, and a number of others. To help move under-employed and unemployed Americans into jobs at Home Depot, they have launched a national partnership with the U.S. Department of Labor. At Home Depot, social responsibility is a priority.

7. TIMBERLAND COMPANY

Timberland is another company with a strong commitment to volunteerism and community service. The company offers all employees forty hours of paid leave time to serve in their communities. It also gives employees a "service sabbatical"—three to six months of paid leave—to develop their professional skills while working with a nonprofit organization. Timberland's Serv-A-Palooza is a day of service for the company's employees around the world. The company's Web site includes a VolunteerMatch feature to match people with appropriate volunteer activities.

8. WALT DISNEY COMPANY

What else would helpful Disney employees be called but "VoluntEARS"? Disney employees have been involved in programs such as the Special Olympics; EARS to You, a campaign to make financial contributions to charitable organizations based on an employee's involvement and time commitment; and the Disney Adventures All-Stars program, which encourages and recognizes volunteerism among children. In January 2005 Disney launched its Here to Volunteer campaign to encourage families to spend time together through community outreach.

9. UNITED PARCEL SERVICE

Employees of UPS have at their fingertips a bank of volunteer opportunities with the company's Neighbor to Neighbor internship program. In 2004 the UPS Foundation initiated a program to help national, regional, state and local organizations work to reduce obesity and improve the nutrition of hungry people in their communities. The foundation also supports programs for increasing literacy skills. In January 2005 UPS donated $3 million in aid to the areas devastated by the tsunamis across Southeast Asia.

10. WACHOVIA CORPORATION

In addition to its many philanthropic activities, Wachovia gives its employees four hours of paid leave each month—or six days per year—for volunteer service in schools and other educational programs, where they serve as tutors, mentors, readers, speakers, and other positions. The company also matches employee contributions to educational institutions through its Education First program.

The Big Store

It's second nature for us to visit a big store in our neighborhood, online, or via a convenient glossy catalog. Big-box department stores and big chain stores are commonplace in the twenty-first century. Here are some stores that tried various gimmicks, gizmos, and ways of getting the piece of the consumer dollar that will always be spent.[1]

1. A&P, NEW YORK, NEW YORK

Formerly known as the Great Atlantic and Pacific Tea Company, A&P appeared in 1859 and is touted as the first chain store in America. The chain as we know it today is a full-fledged grocery store. It actually began as a hide and leather store, and later added tea to its selection. Despite its name, it didn't have a West Coast operation until the early 1900s. Today the chain operates under eleven names, including Farmer Jack, Super Fresh, and Food Emporium.

2. ZION'S CO-OPERATIVE MERCANTILE INSTITUTION, SALT LAKE CITY, UTAH

The first department store was created in 1870. You may think today's heavy-hitting department stores have histories

---

[1] Information gathered from *Famous First Facts*, by Steven Anzovin and Janet Podell (New York: H. W. Wilson, 2000).

that stretch way back in time. Yet none are as old as this one. In the late 1870s Mormon founder Brigham Young brought together a group of community and business leaders in one building for the purpose of community-organized merchandising. The group sold several different categories of merchandise, including clothing, wagons, sewing machines, and carpets. Still in operation today, 51 percent of the store's stock is owned by the Church of Latter Day Saints.

3. GRAND UNION, WAYNE, NEW JERSEY

In the 1940s this company began a method of stocking their merchandise that is found in nearly every modern-day convenience store. Take a soft drink off the shelf at a convenience store and by gravity the slot in which it sits will automatically fill the removed drink with one that slides into its place. While it may seem enterprising, the system was actually in operation in the late 1940s and was called a "Food-O-Mat." At its peak, Grand Union operated over two hundred stores in six states, but the chain folded in 2001.

4. CARSON, PIRIE, SCOTT AND COMPANY, CHICAGO, ILLINOIS

While we have seen Sears Roebuck sell Allstate Insurance, and banks and airports selling life and travel insurance, it was this department store that first tried selling insurance as an add-on to wedding gifts bought through its bridal registry. That was in 1953.

5. GIMBEL BROTHERS, PHILADELPHIA, PENNSYLVANIA

This department store lasted for many years before it dissolved in the latter part of the twentieth century. If a department store can sell insurance, why not sell apartments? Gimbel's sold nearly one million dollars worth of cooperative apartments in 1953 from its furniture showroom section.

6. WOOLWORTH'S, UTICA, NEW YORK

It was about 1878 when Frank Winfield Woolworth began to experiment with the idea of a store that would sell things for "five cents." It was a concept that would feed off the volume and appeal of low-priced merchandise. This was what the working class could afford. He tried his idea in Utica, New York, but the concept didn't catch on until he opened a store in Lancaster, Pennsylvania, where the "five-and-dime" idea worked well.

7. MONTGOMERY WARD, CHICAGO, ILLINOIS

Not long after the introduction of the department store, the mail order store came into existence. Aaron Montgomery Ward began a mail order operation in 1872 with a simple single-sheet catalog on eight-by-twelve-inch paper that was mailed out to potential buyers. It was the beginning of a new era in how Americans would buy merchandise. In fact, in 2001 nearly seventeen billion catalogs from various companies were sent out to consumers.

8. KEEDOOZLE CORPORATION, MEMPHIS, TENNESSEE

The sales scheme of Piggly Wiggly founder Charles Saunders was a fully automated grocery store. Patrons at the store, called Keedoozle, a quirky play on "key does all," viewed merchandise displayed behind glass and inserted a key in a slot for each item they desired. Behind the scenes, the item was conveyed to the cashier at the front, where patrons paid for and received their purchases. The innovation was apparently ahead of its time and never caught on.

9. GIMBEL BROTHERS, NEW YORK, NEW YORK

Even before the department store tried to sell cooperative apartments on its furniture showroom, the store sold art, much of which had belonged to William Randolph Hearst. The artwork sold at a public auction in 1941 that has been called "The Sale of the Century."

10. 7-ELEVEN, DALLAS, TEXAS

It was in 1927 in Dallas, Texas, that the Southland Ice Company started selling blocks of ice to refrigerate food. The company soon added milk, bread, and eggs for sale on Sundays and evenings, when grocery stores were closed. The idea took off and the convenience store boom began. After being born under the name "Tote'm" stores, the chain was renamed 7-Eleven when the stores adopted regular hours from seven in the morning to eleven at night. The chain now has over 26,000 stores operating in the United States and seventeen other countries.

The Corporate Culture

Companies do some cute, innovative, and sometimes-wacky things to build the super culture that makes their employees' minds flourish. Even if you despise corporate balance sheets, financial reporting, and other gobbledygook that may sometimes be a bore, you'll love some of the ways companies attempt to create environment, ambience, and a landscape that directly or indirectly makes the cash register ring.

1. PEPSICO

When Coca-Cola, the main competitor of the Pepsi Generation, launched its "New Coke" back in the 1980s, it flopped like an aluminum can being crushed at a recycling depot. So what did Pepsi do? They gave the whole kit and caboodle at Pepsi the day off!

2. NESTLÉ USA

When you visit an executive at this company, you may have to wait a bit in the lobby. But while you're there, you can sample all the mini Nestlé Crunch bars and Nestlé 100 Grand Bars to your heart's desire. At the receptionist's desk is a large bowl of some of the company's products for the taking. Not a bad way to build a sweet reputation.

3. GE-NBC

Late Night with David Letterman was a top nightly show on NBC. When GE took over the television network, Letterman wanted to go to the GE building in New York City. This was once the headquarters of the corporate giant, though at the time it housed its international trading company staff. Letterman went into the lobby with the intent of meeting a muckety-muck from their new parent and tried to shake hands with the security guard on duty. The guard didn't know what to do and tried to shunt the visitors away. When a handshake was extended, the guard pulled his hand away and wouldn't shake hands. Well, that clip was played over and over again on Letterman with slow motion outtakes and constant replays. It was Letterman humor mixed with the new stuffed-shirt GE culture. That culture didn't always jibe with Letterman culture, but fit better with that of NBC. GE and NBC seemed to coexist peacefully, though, despite their cultural differences. Nevertheless, the program, now named *Late Show with David Letterman*, moved to CBS in 1993, where it remains today.

4. BERKSHIRE HATHAWAY

Warren Buffet's plain and simple mannerism is well reflected in the trademark of his company—a plain and simple approach to everything. The company headquarters wears a plain-Jane look, and is located next to a gas station. Buffet's annual reports use low-budget black-and-white photos. He's a firm believer that the corporate hype is better spent on something else—a corporate dividend. If you're about to strike a deal with Buffet and things are going well, he just may take you out for ice cream to nail the deal down.

5. JOHNSON & JOHNSON

At the company's personal products division, there is a health center that beats all gyms. The facility is open during the day so that employees can work out at their choosing and their own schedule. Exercise classes are led by well-paid instructors and personal trainers, some of whom have a master's degree in human physiology.

6. IBM

If anyone can do it, Big Blue can. The company's cafeteria in Armonk, New York, employs graduates of the nearby Culinary Institute of America. And if you are enthusiastic about golf, you'll find that IBM shares that enthusiasm. They have their own golf course and country club for corporate members and guests.

7. U.S. SMOKELESS TOBACCO COMPANY

Welcome to Greenwich, Connecticut, a commuter town with green grass, quaint little white homes that go for a million-plus, and a population of modern New York City executives on the run. Greenwich was the home of the executive in the 1950s novel *The Man in the Grey Flannel Suit*. It's also the home of the U.S. Smokeless Tobacco Company, which sells the ever-famous smokeless tobacco products like Skoal and Copenhagen snuff. Visit the marketing executives in the company's headquarters, and you'll find them sitting at their desks, but behind each of them is a spittoon. Don't be flabbergasted if during the meeting, the marketing executive turns away to spit into his spittoon. I guess it just comes with the territory.

8. WALT DISNEY COMPANY

When you visit the Disney theme parks, you'll soon realize that they have a unique culture of their own. Disney employees must go through a rigid screening process. Every employee must go through extensive training. The training is an orientation to the Disney way. At Disney, appearances count. The company has rigid grooming standards and ferrets out new hires who might complement its Peter Pan, Huckleberry Finn, or Snow White image. Work for Disney, and you must learn a new vocabulary. The company hopes this will mold a new way of thinking. Customers are "guests." Going to work means going "on stage." Your workday is your "performance." It may seem like fantasy overload, but the company has built an image in the eye of the world that is like no other.

9. CAPITAL ONE

The northern Virginia financial services company is a leading marketer of credit card services. Whatever you do at Capital One, and however you do it, you are measured. The firm uses the horsepower of information technology to measure everything from mean time to hire, to standard deviation of the time you're on the phone with a customer. Being hired in one of Capital One's many call centers means going through an objective set of hoops via phone and computer. Finally, toward the very end of the hiring process, you actually speak to a human being.

10. NORDSTROM'S

The company believes that customer service is its lifeblood. Walk into a Nordstrom's store with a specific product in mind and the sales associate will take a genuine interest in *your* interest. Sales employees have a personal planner or organizer in which they routinely list their contacts, with accompanying notes. "Mrs. Jones, going to Florida, daughter in law school" might read one entry. When Mrs. Jones comes back, the sales associate might ask, "Is Suzie getting ready for the bar exam?" or "So how was the Florida sunshine?" Nordstrom's redefines the concept of "the extra mile," and it seems to work pretty well.

The Oldest Corporations

You may have thought that the RCA Victor label, Cream of Wheat advertisements in women's magazines, and Coca-Cola advertisements on the back of *National Geographic* represent some of the oldest corporations in America. Don't forget that before the days of the Revolutionary War, there was a cadre of merchants, purveyors, artisans, and craftsmen supplying the flow of commerce in the new land. And while a few of these have recently been swallowed up in acquisitions or mergers, many are still ticking today. Here are some firms that are among the oldest corporations still in existence.[1]

1. J. E. RHOADS & SONS (1702)

This company, located in Branchburg, New Jersey, makes conveyor belts and related mill equipment and supplies. It is the oldest company in America. So what specifically does it sell? Well, much of its technology sounds like it came right out of a spare parts supply house for a cotton mill or flour

[1] Information gathered from http://www.cftech.com/BrainBank/ CORPORATEADMINISTRATION/OldestCos.ht ml.

mill: flat power-transmission belting, flour bags, flour bag thread, elevator buckets, and elevator belts.

2. COVENANT LIFE INSURANCE (1717)

You've no doubt heard the old maxim that death and taxes are the only two things we can count on for sure, but apparently Covenant Life discovered that long before our present-day United States was even united, as death was a big part of its business. In 1994 the company's operations came to an end when the Provident Insurance Companies bought it, yet agreed to keep its policies in force. Its base is outside of Philadelphia, Pennsylvania.

3. PHILADELPHIA CONTRIBUTIONSHIP (1752)

This insurance company began in 1752, when Benjamin Franklin joined a group of prominent citizens to establish what is now the oldest property insurance company in the country. Whether "contributionship" is an actual word of the English language didn't matter to Benjamin Franklin, as he named the company the Philadelphia Contributionship for the insurance of houses from loss by fire.

4. DEXTER CORPORATION (1767)

No, it's not the shoe company! Dexter is a global specialty supplier of adhesives and coatings based in Seabrook, New Hampshire. In its evolution as a primitive specialized materials supplier, this company has kept pace with the demands of modern technology. The company has three operating segments: life sciences, non-woven polymers, and specialty polymers, and supplies specialty materials to the aerospace, electronics, food packaging, and medical markets.

5. D. LANDRETH SEED (1784)

This Baltimore, Maryland–based company sold garden seed to George Washington, Thomas Jefferson, James Madison,

and Joseph Bonaparte. The Landreths have been intermit-
tent leaders in the seed industry ever since David Landreth
opened his business on May 21, 1784, upon his arrival from
England.

6. BANK OF NEW YORK (1784)

Founded in 1784 by Alexander Hamilton, this firm lays its
claim as the nation's oldest bank. Today it is one of the
largest financial holding companies in the United States and
provides a complete range of banking and other financial
services to corporations and individuals worldwide.

7. MUTUAL ASSURANCE (1784)

Insurance companies weren't always based in Hartford, Connecticut. Mutual Assurance is yet another Philadelphia insurer that offered fire and homeowners' insurance. It offered
"perpetual" insurance, which was paid through a one-time
up-front deposit. The catch: if the value of the insured property went up, so did the additional premiums.

8. BANK OF BOSTON (1784)

The Bank of Boston began in the same year as the Bank of
New York and thus just misses the title of oldest bank. The
city's harbor and its position at the mouth of three rivers
made it the commercial hub of New England. The Massachusetts bank was founded to finance trade and commerce
activity in the bustling port city of Boston.

9. GEORGE R. RUHL & SONS (1789)

This family-owned firm predates Baltimore's city charter.
Each of its trucks bears the words "George R. Ruhl & Son,
America's Oldest Bakery Supply House, Established 1789."
The company burned to the ground in Baltimore's 1904 fire,
rebounded, and is still alive and well today.

10. **BURNS & RUSSELL (1790)**

It took six generations of the Russell family in Baltimore, Maryland, to make this manufacturer of handmade bricks. Its earliest clay mines were on the present-day site of the Baltimore Orioles' Camden Yards stadium. Burns & Russell's brick and building products are still a mainstay for architects and specifying building engineers.

Banks off the Beaten Path

B anks have always conjured up the image of architec-
tural wonders with iron-barred teller windows, ornate
columns, and palatial décor. But not every bank fits that
mold. Many banks have succeeded in providing everything
from the sublime to the ridiculous—or maybe not so ridiculous when we look at the trends that they started. Some provide enterprising new ways of doing business or serving
customers. Here are ten banks that do just that.[1]

1. EXCHANGE NATIONAL BANK OF CHICAGO (1946)

Exchange National pioneered the first drive-thru bank. The
innovative architecture of the bank was such that ten teller
windows were set up behind bulletproof glass. A car would
drive up to a window. Through a sliding drawer, the transaction was made, and—presto! The drive-thru bank transaction
was complete.

2. CHEMICAL BANK, NEW YORK (1969)

This bank opened the first automatic teller machine, in Rock-
ville Center, New York. At the time of its opening, we had just

[1] Information gathered from *Famous First Facts*, by Steve Anzovin
and Janet Podell (New York: H. W. Wilson, 2000).

sent a man to the moon, and now we were sending bank customers to a bank to do business with a machine. With a precoded card, the machine would dispense a finite sum of money in an envelope. Now it's difficult to imagine life without such a mechanism.

3. SURETY NATIONAL BANK'S CIVIC CENTER BRANCH (1970)

This bank branch was a hybrid of the first automatic teller machine. It used technology to expedite the job of the traditional human bank teller plus provide automatic teller service. The bank wasn't entirely confident that a self-serve window would be problem-free for the customer. It employed a real-life teller who monitored six self-serve stations via a closed–circuit television network.

4. THE BOWERY SAVINGS BANK, NEW YORK (1955)

Long before Joe DiMaggio ever became its spokesperson, the Bowery bank was winning the hearts of the New York rider—train rider, that is. If you think banks were all contained in big buildings, think again. The Bowery put a bullet-proof glass–enclosed bank in the middle of Grand Central Station in 1955. Busy commuters had their first taste of commerce bending over backward to make life easier for those on the go.

5. CHEMICAL BANK, NEW YORK (1972)

Banks have tried almost every gimmick imaginable to build their brand loyalty—from a free toaster when you open an account to free stock trades and a slew of other gizmos and gimmicks. Call it innovative or foolish, but Chemical Bank aired movies on small movie screens at three of its Manhattan branches to those waiting on line. Somehow, the concept never seemed to take off.

6. GRAND FOUNTAIN OF THE UNITED ORDER OF TRUE REFORMERS (1889)

This bank operated in Richmond, Virginia, and was the first bank operated by those of African American descent for use

by the same. Earlier, there had been a bank formed and operated by whites for use by African Americans, but not until
this bank was there one operated for and by African Americans.

7. THE NATIONAL CITY BANK OF NEW YORK (1914)

This was the first U.S. bank to set up shop in a foreign country. In 1913 the Federal Reserve Bank set up legislation that
allowed banks to open branches in foreign countries. The
National City Bank blazed the trail a year later when it
opened up a branch in Buenos Aires, Argentina.

8. FOND DU LAC STATE BANK (1934)

The Federal Deposit Insurance Corporation (FDIC) pre-
serves and promotes public confidence in the U.S. financial
system by insuring deposits in banks and thrift institutions.
In 1934 the Fond du Lac State Bank was the first FDIC-in-
sured bank whose depositors were paid from its insured reserves. The FDIC made $104,000 in payments to those who
had deposited their life savings and lost them to the Great
Depression.

9. SAINT LUKE PENNY SAVINGS BANK (1903)

This bank was not the first bank operated by an African
American; however, it was the first bank founded by and run
by an African American woman. Maggie Lena Walker became the first African American woman president of this
bank.

10. WELLS FARGO BANK (1990)

This California-based bank introduced the world's first online
banking service in 1990. It was not until 1997 that the Nationwide Building Society launched a similar service in the
United Kingdom. Online banking today is a major method of
conducting personal banking business. Since the introduction of the first services, many other banks have started their
own electronic banking services with access available via
personal computer, cell phone, or other mobile computing
device.

THE
CLIMATE

Street-Smart Lexicon

Wall Street speaks a language of its own. The hectic flurry of activity on the trading floor is its own unique culture. It seems that with every unique culture comes a lexicon of slang unique to it. Wall Street is no exception, and here are some of its expressions that you may have heard and wondered about.[1]

1. THE TRIPLE WITCHING HOUR

For the wizards of Wall Street, the triple witching hour occurs on the third Friday of March, June, September, and December. The term refers to the final hour before the market closing when options and futures contracts on stock indices expire on the same day. This simultaneous expiration has been known to create much volatility in options, futures, and their underlying securities.

2. BOTTOM FISHING

This term refers to the speculative but noble act of finding securities that have fallen to their weakest point but never-

[1] Information gathered from *Barron's Dictionary of Finance and Investment Terms*, by John Downes and Jordan Elliot Goodman (Woodbury, NY: Barron's, 1985).

This image, taken in 1865 from a ship's deck,
is the earliest known photograph of Wall Street.

theless show promise to the shrewd speculator. Bottom fish
are often bankrupt and in deplorable condition at first sight.
One bottom fish, out of favor, however, may turn into a trophy fish—that is the credo of the bottom fisher.

3. THE RANDOM WALK THEORY

An inebriated person may walk a line with random abandon-
ment. Such is the theory behind stock prices that follow a
"random walk." The financial gurus of the random walk
school believe that past prices are not predictive of future
price behavior and that such prices are a result of random
emotion in the marketplace. They believe that the true future
price of a stock consists of its intrinsic value plus its dividend
yield. Random walk theorists are in opposition to "techni-
cians," who use charts, graphs, and price behavior under
given conditions to predict the order and pattern of security
prices. Through the years, both groups have had opposing
views on the way things work in the market.

4. A HEAD-AND-SHOULDERS PATTERN

This term has nothing to do with Procter and Gamble's shampoo! When stock prices are plotted on a chart, if the stock has had three successive rallies, the pattern of change can depict the head and shoulders of a person, with the head being the stock's second rise. It is a technical analyst's telltale sign that decline is imminent.

5. ZOMBIE

You've heard of them in the movies, and you may have tried an alcoholic drink named after them, but there's also a Wall Street term that bears this name. A zombie is a company that is operating in a bankrupt or insolvent state awaiting closure, acquisition, or merger. Some zombies may stay zombies for a while. Many just die a miserable death.

6. WINDOW DRESSING

Even financiers use the other side of their brain for some creative, artsy activity. Window dressing refers to the deceptive practice that some mutual fund portfolio managers engage in whereby weak securities and holdings are sold and newfound strong securities are bought. This switch takes place just before the quarterly report or other public disclosure of their holdings in order to give the appearance that the portfolio is robust and prosperous.

7. JANUARY EFFECT

Even the motions of the market can be temperamental. The January effect is a controversial phenomenon that many financial know-it-alls don't agree on. The expression describes a tendency of stocks to perform better between December 31 and the end of the first week in January than at any other time of the year. The explanation is that portfolio managers and other investors have a tendency to oversell their securities in December to establish losses for tax purposes. Some also credit the December selling as a means to allow for holiday spending. Prices then rebound in January as traders buy back the stock, hence the "effect" commented on in financial programs and columns. Many dispute it and don't believe it really happens.

8. TRIPLE BOTTOM

This refers to a pattern whereby security prices have made three bottoms at nearly the same price and have then broken away from their bottom level. The term is commonly used by technical analysts as a sign of new upward movement in a stock's price. It only took three bottoms to reach the conclusion!

9. RULE OF 72

The rule of 72 is a simple but useful benchmark used by anyone involved with any aspect of investing or financing. The rule holds that money invested at 7.2 percent doubles every ten years. It also holds true that money invested at 10 percent doubles every 7.2 years. In general, it is a benchmark that refers to the doubling time on an investment, for which the compounded annual rate of return times the number of years must equal roughly 72 for the investment to double in value. Now, that sounds like an exercise in mathematical gymnastics, but it's often used as financial jargon when referring to compound rates of return.

10. SHORT AGAINST THE BOX

It's hard to figure out what this term means from the way it sounds. Selling short against the box first means to sell a security short while owning the underlying security long. A short sale is one in which you sell it today by borrowing the security with the intent of buying it back at a later date when it is at a lower price. Shorting against the box is a tactic in which the seller owns but does not want to sell long the security that is being held, for tax or other reasons. It'll take you a day of figuring to understand why you'd want to do that, but trust me, it can be a good tactic!

Safety First

If you've ever had anything to do with industrial companies or workplace safety, you may have had the pleasure of learning about the U.S. Department of Labor's Occupational Safety and Health Administration—affectionately known as OSHA. While the industrial branch of a company usually posts their safety record at the entrance to their plant or facility, one shipyard in Louisiana took a different tact. At the entrance to their facility, they posted a sign reading, "If you think OSHA is some town in Wisconsin, please come to the safety office." Workplace safety and accidents are true concerns in the industrial and even nonindustrial workplace. Here are the ten occupational safety standards that firms violate most often.[1]

1. SCAFFOLDING

The OSHA standard is aimed at preventing falls from scaffolds at heights of more than ten feet. You see scaffolding on everything from the Statue of Liberty to tall buildings that Superman used to land on. In New York City they're simply part of the landscape. Among the common abuses of OSHA

[1] Information gathered from www.osha.gov.

scaffolding standards is failure to provide competent people to supervise scaffold decks less than four feet wide. A company that has scaffolding and doesn't live up to OSHA standards is in violation of the code. More firms violate this standard than any other.

2. FALL PROTECTION

This standard protects workers from falls above six feet. Interestingly, in 1998 OSHA granted homeowners an exemption under congressional pressure. What this rule means is that workers must have protection that prevents falls from occurring. The most common problems are missing guards at the open edges of floors and lack of training for workers in this environment. A common fall-related problem is when workers step on insulation and go right through the roof to the floor below.

3. HAZARD COMMUNICATION

Although this standard is very often violated, OSHA requires all employers to develop and implement a written hazard communication program. This means that they must provide written details of the hazards posed by various substances, use appropriate safety labeling for containers, and create safety data sheets. OSHA requires this standard wherever chemicals are used. If chemicals are used in a remote location or are only used sparingly, many firms overlook the safety sheets. Zap! They've now violated a standard, and that's how it became so widely violated.

4. LOCKOUT OR TAGOUT

These are two additional buzzwords for the safety-savvy manager. OSHA requires employers to de-energize electrical equipment for maintenance or post a sign warning that equipment should first be turned off. Employers complain that this is a labor-intensive standard and that requirements are difficult. The "just in case" hazard of an electrical shock means that a very extensive network of electricity must be shut down. As a result, workers bypass lockout procedures to save time—and *zap* again. Not from electricity, but from OSHA, who issues a fine or other slap on the hand.

5. MACHINE GUARDING

This OSHA standard requires employers to place guards over or in front of a machine's moving parts. It sounds reasonable, but all too often the machine guards are removed and not replaced. Often these guards are removed because they are perceived to be "in the way of my work." This does pose a serious threat, and any workplace that allows it will be politely interrupted when an OSHA representative inspects the premises.

6. RESPIRATORY PROTECTION

We finally come to a violation that is self-evident. This standard requires respirator use to protect workers from toxic fumes or other breathing hazards. Workers must monitor the air to determine if they must wear the mask. This can be labor intensive and yet another cumbersome task to worry about. Workers who don't comply with this OSHA standard create a violation and yet another reason to slap the hand of the firm responsible—or is that "irresponsible"?

7. ELECTRICAL WIRING

Electrical equipment, wiring, and insulation require grounding to prevent the hazard of electrical shock. When a machine is not grounded with the correct equipment or devices, the entire live electrical apparatus is a hazard. Also, unused openings in electrical devices must be covered and approved, and specified covers for junctions and electrical boxes must be used in order to avoid violation of this standard.

8. MECHANICAL POWER

This OSHA standard calls for proper guarding of gears, chains, belts, pulleys, and drive shafts so that a worker does not become caught in the transmission devices. This is closely related to the previous problem of absent machine covers, but it hones in on serious machine-guarding hazards. Most common violations involve the failure to guard sprocket wheels and chains, or rotating parts such as belts and pulleys.

9. **POWERED INDUSTRIAL TRUCKS**

It might have been better if the folks at OSHA just called them forklifts, because that's what this standard refers to. If forklifts are floating around the facility and the operators' seat belts aren't buckled, or the drivers are not licensed and trained, then the company is in violation of the standard.

10. **EXCAVATIONS**

This standard covers the failure to shore up trenches and similar construction violations. Common problems are cave-ins, falls, electrocutions, falling objects, and bad air. When employers dig a temporary trench, they often overlook the need to reinforce the trench and provide adequate reinforcement for the area. The short time the trench is in existence doesn't matter to the OSHA inspector, who errs on the side of caution and knows that a life could be lost in no time flat to the open trench that overlooks the requirement of shoring and reinforcement.

Cocktail Conversation for Accountants

Accountants and tax preparers know it all and have all the answers—except when it comes to the history of taxation. Here are ten appetizing tidbits you can stump them on.[1]

1. EARLY REVENUE RAISING

President Lincoln created a revenue-raising measure in 1862. This measure helped to pay for Civil War expenses. It also created the position of Commissioner of Internal Revenue and the first federal income tax in the United States. A 3 percent tax was levied on incomes between $600 and $10,000. A 5 percent tax was levied on incomes of more than $10,000.

2. THE NEAR DEATH OF TAXATION

By 1872 the U.S. government had stopped collecting taxes, but Congress attempted to institute a new income tax plan. In 1895 the United States Supreme Court ruled that the proposed new income tax was unconstitutional because it was a direct tax and not shared or apportioned among the states

[1] Information gathered from www.irs.gov.

according to their population. Federal income taxes were not collected again until 1916, with the passage of the Sixteenth Amendment.

3. TAXATION POWER BY THE GOVERNMENT

We can thank former President Taft for this one. In 1909 Taft urged Congress to propose a constitutional amendment giving government the power to tax incomes without burdening the states according to their population. Congress also levied a 1 percent tax on net corporate incomes of more than $5,000.

4. THE SIXTEENTH AMENDMENT

In 1913, with the threat of World War I looming in the background, the state of Wyoming became the thirty-sixth and last state needed to ratify the Sixteenth Amendment to the Constitution. The amendment stated, "Congress shall have the power to lay and collect taxes on incomes, from whatever source derived, without apportionment among the several states, and without regard to any census or enumeration." Congress would later adapt a 1 percent tax on net personal income of more than $3,000, with a surtax of 6 percent on incomes of more than $500,000.

5. PROHIBITION

In 1919 the states ratified the Eighteenth Amendment. This prohibited the manufacture, sale, or transport of alcoholic beverages or those that would intoxicate. As a result, Congress passed the Volstead Act. This gave the Commissioner of Internal Revenue the responsibility for enforcement of prohibition. Yes, you heard it right—the taxman was monitoring the whiskey wagons. But this was not for long. Some eleven years later, the Department of Justice assumed primary prohibition enforcement duties.

6. "THE GREATEST TAX BILL IN AMERICAN HISTORY"

The Revenue Act of 1942 was proclaimed by President Franklin D. Roosevelt as "the greatest tax bill in American history." The act passed Congress and increased taxes along with the number of Americans subject to the income tax. It also created deductions for medical and investment expenses.

7. FORM 1040 REBORN

The U.S. Congress passed and enacted the Individual Income Tax Act in 1944. This act created the standard deductions on Form 1040.

8. GETTING AL CAPONE

The federal government was determined to catch Al Capone one way or another. The "other" way was in 1931 when the IRS Intelligence Unit used an undercover agent to gather evidence against Capone. He was convicted of tax evasion and sentenced to eleven years.

9. REAGONOMICS

In 1986 President Reagan signed into law the Tax Reform Act. This act was described by many as the most significant piece of tax legislation in thirty years. With some three hundred provisions, the act took three years to implement and established a code of federal tax laws for the third time since the Revenue Act of 1918.

10. THE DIGITAL AGE

Click and send. The day finally arrived in 1992 when taxpayers who owed money were allowed—even encouraged—to file returns electronically.

Valuable Stock (Certificates)

*S*cripophily. No, it's not an exotic forensic science or some other esoteric field of research popular in academia. Scripophily is the name for following and collecting old or valuable stock or bond certificates. The certificates are in demand not for their market value, but rather for their aesthetic or other desired characteristics. If you ever want to learn a bit more about scripophily, visit Scripophily.com and you'll find a great Web site with rare stock certificate offerings. It's a key place to buy stock certificates with some interesting history behind them. Here's a sampling of what a scripophile might be interested in.

1. **THE NORTH EUROPEAN OIL CORPORATION**

This company offered a small-issue penny stock around the time of the Great Depression, and many who held the certificates thought the company faded away. The company was revamped under a new name in 1957 when an unknown oil reserve was tapped in nearby properties. Stockholders who may have shares lingering in the back of an old file cabinet would find that they have appreciated in value by one thousand fold. There are still some one million shares floating around out there.

2. THE BUCKEYE STEEL CASTINGS COMPANY

According to Scripophily.com, an old certificate from this company is no ordinary collectible stock certificate from the 1920s. If you could get your hands on any of these certificates of this day, you'd find that it is hand-signed by Samuel Prescott Bush, the great-grandfather of President George W. Bush.

3. ENRON

One certificate that Scripophily.com has in its collection and offers for sale is a "priceless" share of Enron stock. The certificate has printed signatures of the company's officers, including the infamous Kenneth L. Lay as chairman of the board, who later resigned and was often the focal point of much of the scandal behind a company accused of fraudulent accounting practices. A once-bustling company, Enron's stock today is deemed worthless.

4. THE PAN MOTOR COMPANY

This stock certificate is adorned with drawings of an open touring car and a hood ornament with the company president's name, Pandolfo, and a hubcap with the company's name, "PAN." What you may not know by looking at the stock certificate is that the founder of this company, Samuel Conner Pandolfo, was a scam artist who put up a front as a full-scale auto manufacturer. The company folded in 1922 and produced only 737 cars in the four years that it existed.

5. HALOID

The name of this company sounds like some odd chemical compound. The truth is, it was chartered in 1906 and took on a more recognizable name in 1961: Xerox. Had you come across one of these rare specimen certificates, you would be about $1 million richer today. Not a bad find, *if* you can find it.

6. **PLANET HOLLYWOOD**

Planet Hollywood was formed by an investing syndicate of Hollywood celebrities. Collectible stock certificates of this company include signatures by Arnold Schwarzenegger, Demi Moore, Bruce Willis, and Sylvester Stallone. A stock certificate isn't the typical place to find their signatures. But these aren't the typical signatures you'd find on a stock certificate either.

7. **AMERICAN EXPRESS**

An early share certificate of this company stock includes the signature of one of its cofounders, William Fargo—yes, the man of rootin'-tootin' stagecoach fame. The certificate is over 143 years old and is said to command about $750 for

Museum of American Financial History

This collectible stock certificate from the 1870s was for shares of the American Merchants Union Express Company, better known today as American Express.

its collectible value. Although American Express always says, "Don't leave home without it," if you find one of these certificates, you might just want to leave it at home—or better yet, in a safe deposit box.

8. WEBVAN

You may recall it as a failed dot-com company that had tried to revolutionize the grocery industry. But the share that sold on the open market near its collapse for about eleven cents sold on e-Bay in 2001 for over $100. Why? Not exactly for its aesthetic value, but for the anticipated value of the certificate being a landmark of the unforgettable dot-com boom. Also in the arena of failed dot-com stocks are eToys.com and Dr. Koop.com. Have any? Hold on to 'em.

9. HOUDINI MOTION PICTURES

This was the movie and film company of the famous escape artist Harry Houdini. The certificate was signed by the grand master himself. Despite its $10 face value, the stock certificate is said to be worth about $4,500. Of course, value is in the eyes of the beholder.

10. NEW JERSEY JUNCTION RAILROAD CO.

This 1886 certificate was issued when J. P. Morgan was in competition with the other magnates of the day: Rockefeller and Vanderbilt. Their railroads were fierce rivals. Unique to this certificate is that it shows Morgan's yacht, the *Corsair*. The yacht is where the magnates met to discuss the possibility of combining their rail lines and jacking up rail prices. It was aboard the yacht that someone asked Morgan how much his vessel cost. He replied, "If you have to ask, you can't afford it." A new expression was born! What history behind that certificate.

Jobs to Watch

*C*apital and *labor.* If you've ever taken an economics course, you know that the two words are an integral part of economics. Labor changes over time. The number of people change. The standards of labor change. The wages associated with labor change. What also changes is the demand for labor, more specifically, the demand for certain labor functions. Some jobs are just in huge demand at any given time. The U.S. Department of Labor monitors the demand for labor and puts out forecasts for the demand for labor occupations based over time. When the department looked at the jobs that are likely to have the most growth from 2000 to 2010, here's what they found.[1]

1. COMPUTER SOFTWARE ENGINEERS FOR APPLICATIONS

Well, it should come as no surprise that the information boom may be suppressed at times, but overall it is still humming. As we rely more and more on software applications, we need many software engineers to design, build, and implement the applications of that software. As such, by the

[1] Information gathered from www.dol.gov.

year 2010 the number of jobs with this title should be double what is was in 2000.

2. COMPUTER SUPPORT SPECIALISTS

Once software is designed and implemented, it is used. Mainframe computers, wireless devices, routers, servers, and all the many components that make up information technology need to be attended to. A myriad of professionals who fall into the category of computer support specialists need to be available. This career path is estimated to grow by 97 percent by the year 2010.

3. COMPUTER SOFTWARE ENGINEERS FOR SYSTEMS SOFTWARE

Software that incorporates large systems and networks requires a more specific knowledge of computer engineering. This computer engineer is more concerned about the software performance for the entire system rather than its performance for a specific application. This profession is slated to grow by 90 percent by 2010.

4. NETWORK AND COMPUTER SYSTEMS ADMINISTRATORS

Further along the information technology growth line are the administrators who keep all the bells and whistles operating. This is a bit different from computer support specialists in that it's very specific work that requires knowledge of a specific network or system. These jobs are estimated to grow by 82 percent by the year 2010.

5. NETWORK SYSTEMS AND DATA COMMUNICATIONS ANALYSTS

Specifically, this profession will be increasingly critical as analysts play more of a strategic planning role in ensuring that the systems and data are best used to the advantage of the organization. They figure out just how networks and data communications shall be used. This profession is slated to grow by 77 percent by 2010.

6. DESKTOP PUBLISHERS

Well, we're still in information technology, but in a profession that you may not have suspected would be on this list. A desktop publisher somewhere behind the scenes produces almost everything in print. The information technology revolution has meant that anything and everything published is done by some digital means. Behind that means are layout artists, production artists, and designers who use desktop publishing software and equipment to produce the product. This profession is estimated to grow by 67 percent by 2010.

7. DATABASE ADMINISTRATORS

Data is the stuff that information technology manipulates. Data is sacred and is stored and backed and must be attended to by snap-to analysts who can ensure that the data used is just right for the horsepower of the network technology. Data changes. Data can't be lost. Data is—well, to many an organization—everything! Because of the importance of data, it must be managed and administered properly; hence, the newfound profession of database administrator. This profession is slated to grow by 66 percent by the year 2010.

8. PERSONAL AND HOME CARE AIDES

Finally we reach a top-ten growth profession that's not in the information technology arena. Baby boomers are approaching retirement age. There should be a critical growth in the elder population in the not-so-distant future. As such, this profession is slated to grow by 62 percent by 2010.

9. COMPUTER SYSTEMS ANALYSTS

While many of these computer-oriented professions sound alike, a computer systems analyst is someone who figures out how to best utilize a computer system to achieve the desired results. This profession is slated to grow by 60 percent by 2010.

10. **MEDICAL ASSISTANTS**

With the aging of our population coupled with the rising cost of health care, medical assistants are viewed as a growing profession. Medical assistants may also be taking the place of physicians for many routine procedures as the number of illnesses and injuries rise against a more limited supply of physicians. This profession should also increase close to 60 percent by 2010.

Precursors
to Progress

The United States was at a pivotal point around the turn of the twentieth century. During that time period, there was notable industrial and societal progress being made, and the state of the nation was robust. This general time period is often referred to as the "Age of Progress." Here are ten events that shaped this time of progress and prosperity.[1]

1. CARNEGIE GIVES MONEY TO BUILD LIBRARIES (MARCH 12, 1901)

Andrew Carnegie was one of the wealthiest industrialists. His fortune was derived from entering into an emerging niche of steel making in the shadow of the industrial revolution. Carnegie believed in giving back to the world with the same generosity that gave him his fortune as a steel maker. And he did it in a big way! On March 12, 1901, the Scottish immigrant offered the city of New York $5.2 million for the construction of sixty-five branch libraries. Carnegie went on to use his fortune to build more libraries, schools, and public foundations. Carnegie's act would pave the way for great

[1] Information gathered from www.loc.gov.

philanthropists to redistribute their wealth in magnanimous gestures such as building libraries and other entities for the benefit of all. The fruits of progress enabled many of the great business leaders who made advancements to share their wealth through philanthropic efforts.

2. THE AVAILABILITY AND USE OF COAL AS A POWER SOURCE (LATE 1800s)

The Industrial Revolution took place in the late nineteenth century. It was characterized by social and economic change caused by technological advances and the switch in manufacturing from the work of humans to machines. At this time, coal was widely used to heat buildings; however, it was also burned to power steam engines used in manufacturing and locomotion and to power almost all of the innovations of the Industrial Revolution.

3. WILBUR AND ORVILLE WRIGHT'S FIRST FLIGHT (DECEMBER 17, 1903)

"For some years, I have been afflicted with the belief that flight is possible to man. My disease has increased in severity and I feel that it will soon cost me an increased amount of money if not my life." Three years after Wilbur Wright wrote those words, he and his brother, Orville, put their belief in flight to the test in Kill Devil Hills, North Carolina. With the advent of flight, there was a new vision for travel and trade and the possibility that not only could cities and states connect with each other, but continents could do so as well.

4. CAMERAMAN FRED A. DOBSON BEGAN FILMING *THE SKYSCRAPERS OF NEW YORK* (NOVEMBER 8, 1906)

In 1906 cameraman Fred A. Dobson made a bit of history that Americans decades later would come to cherish—the moving pictures. In November of that year, Dobson filmed *The Skyscrapers of New York*. The set was an actual uncompleted skyscraper at Broadway and Twelfth Street. Well, the plot might not have been so exciting: a construction foreman fires a crewmember for fighting, only to have the angry employee turn to stealing to put bread on the table. But the film proved that this progressive age was one when Americans sought enjoyment in their everyday lives, and movies were and still are a way to do that.

5. NEW YORK SUBWAY SYSTEM OPENED FOR BUSINESS (OCTOBER 27, 1904)

In London it's the Tube; in Paris it's the Métro; and in New York City it's the subway. On Thursday afternoon, October 27, 1904, the mayor of New York City, George B. McClellan, officially opened the New York City subway system. The first subway train left City Hall station with the mayor at the controls and arrived twenty-six minutes later at 145th Street. The subway opened to the general public at 7 P.M. that evening, and before the night was over, 150,000 passengers had ridden the trains through the underground tunnels. Within a city, there was now a mobility that made the entire city accessible to the masses.

6. A PERMANENT TAX DAY (APRIL 15, 1913)

When the country was young, it struggled to raise funds from the thirteen original states—$15 million from each state in 1779 and more in following years. The government collected the first income tax during the Civil War, but only temporarily. President Grover Cleveland tried to start up regular yearly income taxes in 1895, but the U.S. Supreme Court ruled it unconstitutional. For supporters of the income tax that meant amending the Constitution, which the government finally did in 1913 with the Sixteenth Amendment. From that point on, Congress could legally collect taxes on incomes.

7. RAILWAY TO THE FLORIDA KEYS (JANUARY 22, 1912)

In the early 1900s Henry M. Flagler, a Florida developer, decided a train would be a practical way for people to get to the island of Key West, Florida. To complete the railway, forty-two bridges had to be constructed. The length of track connected mainland Florida to the southernmost settlement in the United States and the small keys (islands) in between. On January 22, 1912, Flagler boarded the first train of the Florida East Coast Railway bound for Key West. Railroad construction such as this opened up new avenues of trade and travel.

8. THE EXPEDITION ACT WAS PASSED (FEBRUARY 11, 1903)

J. P. Morgan's U.S. Steel Corporation controlled all the stages of steel production from iron-ore mining to steel manufacturing. When one company has such strong control over an industry, it makes it difficult for others to compete. Critics of companies like U.S. Steel Corporation said that allowing a company to control so many aspects of an industry hurt the general public. By 1902 there was such concern about huge "trusts" like U.S. Steel that President Theodore Roosevelt ordered the Justice Department to use "antitrust" laws to prosecute not only the steel industry trust but also the meatpacking, oil, and railroad trusts. He said that these industries took advantage of the public by limiting competition. As a result, the Expedition Act was passed on February 11, 1903, making antitrust suits a high priority in the nation's legal system. Roosevelt quickly gained a reputation for breaking up trusts. From this act, many other regulations were passed and instituted to promote a more competitive market in the U.S. economy.

9. THE FIRST IMMIGRANT LANDED ON ELLIS ISLAND (JANUARY 1, 1892)

More than 12 million people entered the United States through the Ellis Island immigration center from 1892 to 1954. For sixty-two years people came to Ellis Island from

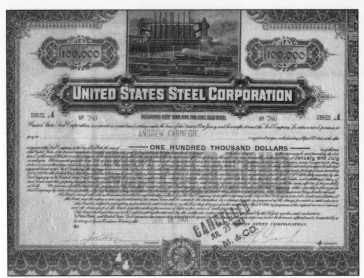

Museum of American Financial History

This $100,000 bond was part of the $20 million in bonds issued to Andrew Carnegie in 1901 when J. P. Morgan engineered the deal that brought U.S. Steel into existence. This remains one of the most important and impressive deals in American business history.

around the world because they wanted to become American citizens. After the boats docked, immigrants would disembark and walk into the registry room, where they would see doctors who would examine them for physical problems and officers who would look over their legal documents. Once they were given the go-ahead to enter, the immigrants were allowed into the United States. A huge inflow of immigrants provided a source of unskilled, cheap labor during the early boom of the industrial revolution. It also produced a generation of hungry and ambitious self-starters who would go on to start businesses and lead America as an industrial powerhouse through the twenty-first century.

10. THE INVENTION OF THE ICE CREAM CONE (JULY 23, 1904)

Would you rather eat rich, delicious ice cream from a bowl or from a cone? On July 23, 1904, the choice became available when Charles E. Minches of St. Louis, Missouri, developed the idea of filling a pastry cone with ice cream, and the ice cream cone was invented. The walk-away cone made its debut later that year at the St. Louis World's Fair.

Busted Flat

O ne can't really have much interest in business without hearing about bankruptcy, failure, and the terrible truth about what business risk sometimes brings. Here are ten people who experienced business failure at some point in their climb to notoriety. You'll notice that failure wasn't always at the beginning, and sometimes it came at the very end.

1. **P. T. BARNUM (1910–1891)**

The circus showman who developed the Greatest Show on Earth actually filed for bankruptcy in 1871 when a few of his business ventures, which included a boardinghouse and a grocery store, went down the drain. Fortunately for ladies and gentlemen and children of all ages, it wasn't until after his failure in business that he actually started and organized his circus idea. In 1881 he began a partnership with James A. Bailey to form the Barnum and Bailey Circus.

2. **MARK TWAIN (SAMUEL CLEMENS) (1835–1910)**

Though his greatest accomplishments are his legends of American literature, the humorist and author lost almost all of his money in a machine called the Paige Compositor, which was an innovative typesetting machine. However, he didn't lose his big home in Hartford, Connecticut, and lectured abroad to pay his way out of debt. Despite the setback, Twain produced some very successful works of literature and earned a place in history as a witty writer of utmost ability and entertainment.

3. MATHEW BRADY (1823–1896)

The famed Civil War photographer, who documented much of the first war in which photography was prevalent, filed for bankruptcy in 1872. He was forced to do so after demand for his photos fell and he found himself unable to keep up with his debts. Nevertheless, Brady bounced back after the U.S. government purchased much of his collection, which allowed him to get back in the groove of selling his photography.

4. HENRY J. HEINZ (1844–1919)

In nearly every restaurant in America and beyond, you can find the Heinz name not too far from the serving table. The ketchup, pickles, relish, and other condiments this entrepreneur sold may be known around the world today; however, there were definite glitches in his company's progress. When the company ran into a bad scenario in 1875 over an unsuccessful crop, it filed for bankruptcy. Ketchup actually wasn't introduced until after this bankruptcy.

5. MILTON HERSHEY (1857–1945)

"Hershey, the great American chocolate bar" was the creation of Milton Hershey, who never got past the fourth grade. His success didn't exactly come easy. In fact, he started four candy companies unsuccessfully. It wasn't until after his bankruptcy that he founded the Hershey's Foods Corporation.

6. HENRY FORD (1863–1947)

Today we know his company as the wheels that turn America, yet most people may not know that Ford's first two automobile manufacturing companies failed. It seems to be a trend that success comes to those who persist.

7. JOHNNY UNITAS (1933–2002)

Known as the "Golden Arm," Johnny Unitas's forte was football, but the record-setting Hall of Famer also tried his hand at a variety of businesses, ranging from real estate to bowling alleys and restaurants. His football finesse wasn't enough to make his businesses succeed, and he filed for bankruptcy with each of his businesses. On September 11, 2002, at the age of sixty-nine, the legendary football player died of a heart attack.

8. THOMAS JEFFERSON (1743–1826)

So much in the history books is written about Jefferson, from his agricultural interests and developments, his presidency, and on to being his own architect of his famed home named Monticello. He was a planter, diplomat, musician, scientist, and inventor, as well as an advocate of public education. He was also the founder of the University of Virginia and the greatest patron of learning and the arts in his generation. Though he lived for eighty-three years, it's not always highlighted that due partly to the depressed condition of the day's money market, Jefferson died penniless and bankrupt.

9. ROBERT HARLEY, 1ST EARL OF OXFORD (1661–1724)

In 1711 Harley created the South Sea Company, which had a plan to convert ten million pounds of British government war debt from the War of Spanish Succession into its own shares, with the intent that speculators would invest in the shares. The company would receive annual interest payments from the government and a monopoly on trade with the South Seas and South America. But the situation didn't go exactly as planned. The price of South Sea rose and topped 1,050 pounds in late June of 1720. Only two months later the stock fell by 75 percent, and the venture was considered a fraudulent scam, going down in history as the South Sea Bubble.

10.   STAN LEE (1922–   )

Born Stanley Lieber, the veteran comic artist and creator was one of the founding fathers of Marvel Comics. His creative works included Spiderman, the Hulk, and the Fantastic Four. He later veered off in his own ventures with Stan Lee Media, which went belly up in 2001.

The Organization of Labor

Supply and demand are the two inputs into the proverbial theory of the firm according to microeconomists. What convolutes economic theory is the human side of the worker and his or her "I'm not gonna stand for this" position that labor began to adopt at the turn of the twentieth century. Here are ten events that helped shape organized labor into its present state—for better or for worse.

1. THE ANTHRACITE COAL STRIKE (1902)

The United States relied on coal to power commerce and industry, and anthracite or "hard coal" was essential for domestic heating. Pennsylvania miners had left the anthracite fields, demanding wage increases, union recognition, and an eight-hour workday. As winter approached, public anxiety about fuel shortages and the rising cost of all coal pushed President Theodore Roosevelt to take unprecedented action. When he met with miners and coalfield operators in Washington on October 3, 1902, Roosevelt became the first president to personally intervene and mediate a labor dispute. The strike was resolved after about five months.

2. THE HAYMARKET AFFAIR (1886)

The scuffle arose when a series of violent strikes waged by
railway workers tarnished the union's reputation. On May 4,
police were called in when fighting broke out between striking workers and strikebreakers at the McCormick Reaper
Works of the McCormick Harvesting Machine Company in
the Haymarket area of Chicago. In the confusion, police shot
two union men; later, an explosion killed seven policemen.
Although the person who set off the bomb was never identi-
fied, four alleged anarchist labor leaders were convicted of
conspiracy to commit murder and hanged. Three more remained imprisoned until pardoned by Illinois governor John
Peter Altgeld in 1893. The Haymarket Riot branded as "radical" the eight-hour-day movement and diminished popular
support for organized labor.

3. THE FORMATION OF THE UNITED FARM WORKERS
ORGANIZING COMMITTEE (UFWOC) (AUGUST 22, 1966)

When the National Farm Workers Association (NFWA) and
the Agricultural Workers Organizing Committee (AWOC)
were both engaged in strikes by California grape growers,
the two organizations joined together. The newly formed
union called itself the United Farm Workers of America
(UFW) and took on the heroic leadership of Cesar Chavez
and Dolores Huerta. The UFW went on to gain many conces-
sions for oppressed immigrant farmworkers.

4. THE FIRST CELEBRATION OF LABOR DAY (SEPTEMBER
5, 1882)

On this day, some ten thousand workers assembled in New
York City to participate in America's first Labor Day parade.
After marching from City Hall to Union Square, the workers
and their families gathered in Reservoir Park for a picnic, a
concert, and speeches. This first Labor Day celebration was
initiated by Peter J. McGuire, a carpenter and labor union
leader who one year earlier cofounded the Federation of Or-

ganized Trades and Labor Unions, a precursor of the American Federation of Labor.

5. THE PULLMAN RAIL STRIKE (1893)

The Pullman Rail Company was thought to exploit workers by cutting their pay and laying them off despite raising the rates of those traveling by rail. Rail workers throughout the nation refused to work on trains with Pullman cars. Federal troops were called in to quell the strike, using the Sherman Antitrust Act and U.S. postal laws as justification for intervention.

6. THE AIR TRAFFIC CONTROLLERS STRIKE (1981)

On August 3, 1981, federal air traffic controllers began a nationwide strike after their union rejected the government's final offer for a new contract. According to the law, federal workers could not launch such a strike, and the thirteen thousand striking controllers were issued a back-to-work order. When many of the workers defied the order and did not return to work, they were dismissed by President Ronald Reagan.

7. U.S. POSTAL LETTER CARRIERS WALKOUT (1970)

At the time, it was the first work stoppage in the history of the U.S. Postal Service. Letter carriers in Brooklyn and Manhattan walked off their jobs, and later included some 750,000 postal employees nationwide in solidarity. The action stifled mail delivery in New York, Detroit, and Philadelphia. President Richard Nixon activated militiamen to keep the mail flowing, and the uprising was settled some two weeks later.

8. THE LUDLOW STRIKE (1914)

This was one of the most dramatic confrontations between the capital of the corporation and its labor. The official call to go on strike read: "All mineworkers are hereby notified that a strike of all the coal miners and coke oven workers in

Colorado will begin on Tuesday, September 23, 1913. . . .
We are striking for improved conditions, better wages, and
union recognition. We are sure to win." The state militia fired
machine guns into the tent city of workers who operated the
mines of the Rockefeller-owned Colorado Fuel and Iron
Company in Ludlow, Colorado. Twenty men, women, and
children were killed in what came to be known as "the Ludlow Massacre." The strike began in 1913 and lasted into
1914.

9. THE EXECUTION OF JOE HILL (1915)

Joe Hill was a Swedish immigrant who arrived in Utah in
1913 to work at the Park City silver mines. He became a
labor organizer and union activist, as well as a prominent
member in the radical labor group known as the Industrial
Workers of the World. In 1914 Hill was accused of murdering
a Salt Lake City storeowner, which labor organizers believed
was a plot of the power-wielding "Copper Bosses" of Utah to
attempt to eliminate him. President Woodrow Wilson inter-
vened twice in an attempt to prevent the execution, but Hill
was shot to death by a firing squad at the Utah State Prison
in Sugar House, Utah, on November 19, 1915.

10. THE HOMESTEAD STEEL STRIKE (JUNE 29, 1892)

This labor dispute involved workers belonging to the Amal-
gamated Association of Iron and Steel Workers who worked
at the Carnegie Steel Company at Homestead, Pennsylvania—a steel town that was in existence to produce steel for
the Carnegie empire. The workers were protesting a proposed wage cut, and Henry C. Frick, the company's general
manager, was sent to break the strikers by hiring independent "detectives" from the Pinkerton security agency. The
dispute became bloody and led the state governor to activate
the state militia. The dispute was eventually resolved; however, it is believed that the incident weakened the unionism
of the steel industry at that time.

neither a Borrower nor a Lender Be

Yeah, right. Tell that to the federal government, which has always maintained a level of public debt that will shake the decimal point right out of your pen. Debt has always been a regular vehicle of capitalism. Borrow to pay for things that will eventually catch up to and exceed your debt. It sounds good for a profit-seeking enterprise, but when the federal government does it, watch out! Take a look at how the public debt has grown over the last forty-five years or so, and you'll get a feel for how powerful a runaway freight train can be as it runs down a track out of control.[1]

1. **DECEMBER 30, 1955: $280,768,553,188.96**

Well, the rebuilding didn't mean that the debt wouldn't stay on the books. But heck, at the end of 1955 it was $23 billion over what it had been in the previous five years. The country was still in a rebuilding mode after the end of World War II. But it was also building a tremendous amount of debt.

2. **DECEMBER 30, 1960: $290,216,815,241.68**

By this time the country hadn't gotten out of public debt. But a jump of 10 billion in five years was better than the $23

---

[1] Information gathered from www.publicdebt.treas.gov.

billion increase in the previous five-year period. The baby
boom was in full swing. Housing was scarce. America was
coming out of a "rock around the clock" and "I like Ike" era
and starting to look forward to a JFK administration.

3. DECEMBER 31, 1965: $320,904,110,042.04

So much for the modest $10 billion jump over the previous
five years. Now the debt had increased by a solid $30 billion.
JFK was gone. The civil rights movement was in progress.
America was racing to be the first on the moon. And the nation's debt just kept climbing.

4. DECEMBER 31, 1970: $389,158,403,690.26

By the end of 1970 America was cooking with debt—$79
billion more than just five years before. Man had now walked
on the moon. Vietnam was in full swing, and things weren't
looking good. And the debt continued.

5. DECEMBER 31, 1975: $576,649,000,000.00

You've heard about the power of compounding, and after
you look at what happened to the debt between 1970 and
1975, you can't help but believe it. Between 1965 and 1970
many may have squawked about a $79 billion increase in
public debt. What were they supposed to do now? An increase of over $186 billion dollars from 1970 to 1975 is
enough to say something was getting out of control. Somebody needed to step in and take some action.

6. DECEMBER 31, 1980: $930,210,000,000.00

Well, that somebody was nobody! The years 1975 to 1980
saw one of the largest jumps in the national debt's previous
twenty-year history—over $353 billion!

7. DECEMBER 31, 1985: $1,945,941,616,459.88

Take back everything anyone ever said about an increase in
the public debt before 1985. Between 1980 and 1985 the
public debt just about doubled. The rule of 72 says that

money invested at 7 percent doubles every ten years. Well, this period followed the rule of doubling in five years. Debt in the trillions had arrived.

8.   SEPTEMBER 28, 1990: $3,233,313,451,777.25

Okay, so the government had stopped doubling its debt every five years, but it still was increasing at record speeds. A sign was erected at the entrance to New York's Midtown Tunnel that shows the public debt on a digital scoreboard, with the last digit racing out of control. Every second of time passage means an increase in the public debt.

9.   SEPTEMBER 29, 1995: $4,973,982,900,709.39

You know you're in trouble when you sigh in relief that the debt increase over the past five years was not so bad because it was only $1.7 trillion! But the percentage increase was actually less than in most previous five-year periods. Looking good?

10.   SEPTEMBER 29, 2000: $5,674,178,209,886.86

A trillion here, a trillion there . . . pretty soon we're talking real money. The public debt has had some good five-year stints and some bad ones. But there's only one thing we can conclude about public debt: it will continue to go up.

Dot Cons

For centuries, snake oil salesman and manipulative opportunists have been trying to sell their wares for a quick, easy buck. Since the evolution of the Internet, the mechanism of making the quick, easy buck got easier. The Federal Trade Commission receives reams of complaints regarding the Internet from consumers who have been jilted in some way from scams and cons. In fact, as you read this, you probably have some spam sitting in the inbox of your e-mail program. It seems the desire to scam and con has been around for centuries. Modern-day scams just take on a new form, shape, and place—cyberspace. Here are the Federal Trade Commission's top ten types of "dot cons."[1]

1. INTERNET AUCTIONS

Consumers are lured to the convenience of an online "virtual marketplace." Such a shopping site offers ample selection of products at great deals, purchased through a system of competitive online bidding. The "con" occurs when consum-

---

[1] Information gathered from www.ftc.gov/bcp/conline/pubs/online/dotcons.htm.

ers send their money and then receive an item that is less valuable than described. In some instances, they get nothing at all.

2. INTERNET ACCESS SERVICES

Cash a check and receive free money. Oh, buyers beware. Many consumers have been baited into long-term contracts for Internet access or some other related Web service. What they find is that they face big penalties for cancellation or early termination of the service they have "purchased" by cashing the check.

3. INTERNATIONAL MODEM DIALING

In this scam consumers are offered free access to adult material, simply by downloading a "viewer" program. Those who try it are hit up with sizeable long-distance charges on their phone bill. The program actually disconnects the consumer's modem on a dial-up connection and then reconnects it through an international long distance number.

4. WEB CRAMMING

In this fraudulent offer, consumers get a custom-designed Web site for a free thirty-day trial period and are told they have no obligation to continue. But the "no obligation" is hardly that. They find that their phone bills have been charged or they receive a separate invoice. In some cases this occurs after they have discontinued the trial period. So much for no obligation!

5. MULTILEVEL MARKETING PLANS/PYRAMIDS

Although this scam goes on every day, people continue to fall for it and lose money. The offer is to make money through the products and services you sell as well as through your "downline" (people you recruit to sell under you). The result is that participants wind up buying product without selling to end-users, but instead only to distributors. Eventually the pyramid of distributors fizzles and participants have a garage full of water purifiers, skin cream, or other over-priced paraphernalia.

6. TRAVEL AND VACATION

In this "dot con" the offer is a fanfare trip with all the fringe extras at a bargain-basement price. In reality, the scammers deliver low-quality travel accommodations or no trip at all. Reports also indicate that some people who have fallen for the offers are hit with hidden charges. The whole fiasco ends up being a trip to nowhere.

7. BUSINESS OPPORTUNITIES

Be your own boss and earn big bucks. Yeah, right. Such business opportunities can be quite seductive; however, they often turn out to be a giant flop as a result of unrealistic expectations. Being your own boss with little effort and time is so darn alluring, the scam continues to work day after day, week after week, decade after decade.

8. INVESTMENTS

Day trading, commodities trading, stock market secrets—such offers are alluring to the unknowing consumer who falls for a get-rich-quick promise: make an initial investment and quickly realize huge returns. Many thousands of dollars have gone by the wayside to programs that claim to be able to predict the market or provide some other exaggerated system.

9. HEALTH CARE PRODUCTS/SERVICES

In this scam, health care products and services are not sold through traditional suppliers but rather through direct mail. Such products are touted as surefire cures for serious health problems. The unknowing put their faith in such products and services only to find that they do nothing at all. If it sounds too good to be true, it usually is!

10. **CREDIT CARD SHARING**

It sounds like a dangerous practice and it is. Consumers are offered the ability to surf the Internet and view adult images online for free. There's just one catch: they must share their credit card number to prove that they are over eighteen. In the end, fraudulent promoters wind up using those credit card numbers to run up charges.

Employment and the Law

Employment has always been a key ingredient in economic theory and practice. It's the livelihood that the United States of America has built its prosperity upon and, as such, has always been subject to governmental regulation. Here are ten employment acts of the past seventy-plus years that have shaped and preserved employment protections in the United States.[1]

1. DAVIS-BACON ACT (1931)

This act fought the back-stabbing ways of wage slashing by setting levels for wages on federal construction projects at the prevailing local rates for various labor disciplines.

2. FAIR LABOR STANDARDS ACT (1938)

This act, administered by the Department of Labor, set a minimum wage of twenty-five cents per hour and a maximum workweek of forty hours for most workers in manufacturing. The forty-hour workweek has not changed over the years. The minimum wage level, however, has risen steadily

[1] Information gathered from www.dol.gov.

since that time. The coverage has widened to include most salaried workers and not just manufacturing workers.

3. NATIONAL LABOR RELATIONS ACT (1935)

Known as the Wagner Act, this legislation gave federal sanction to workers' rights to be able to organize and bargain collectively. In addition, the act established an independent National Labor Relations Board to oversee representation elections and act to resolve labor disputes.

4. TAFT-HARTLEY ACT (1945)

This act was designed to place several restrictions on labor unions. Such restrictions included the ending of the "closed shop," whereby workers had to join the union in order to be hired. It also prohibited the president from ordering "cooling off" periods for strikes deemed to imperil the nation's safety.

5. EQUAL PAY ACT (1963)

This act is actually a subpart of the Fair Labor Standards Act of 1938. It is administered and enforced by the Equal Employment Opportunity Commission. It prohibits gender-based wage discrimination between men and women in the same establishment who are performing under similar working conditions.

6. ECONOMIC OPPORTUNITY ACT (1964)

This act was originally intended to help unemployed fourteen- to twenty-one-year-old youths from poor families in gaining work experience and earning income while completing high school. By the end of the 1960s the program had helped over 1.5 million young people. There were three main components to this federally funded program: one for in-school youth; one for out-of-school, unemployed youth; and a summer component for both groups. Local nonprofit sponsors such as public schools, hospitals, and libraries administered the program. The youth worked in public service jobs such as aides in libraries, schools, and museums. The act also helped to establish the Head Start, Job Corps, and Neighborhood Youth Corps programs.

7. OCCUPATIONAL SAFETY AND HEALTH ACT (1971)

Under this law, the secretary of labor sets and enforces safety and health standards for all work environments. Beginning in the Johnson administration, the act underwent years of congressional debate over whether the Department of Labor should administer the law or whether an independent agency should administer it. The final legislation gave the department power to set and enforce standards; however, there was to be a separate review commission to oversee enforcement. The Occupational Safety and Health Administration (OSHA) was established to implement the law.

8. EMPLOYEE RETIREMENT INCOME SECURITY ACT (ERISA) (1974)

This act came about to protect the retirement benefits of American workers. It also was aimed at improving their opportunities to participate in pension plans. Under the act, the Department of Labor is responsible for overseeing the proper management of one million pension plans. Such plans must be managed soundly and for the benefit of the participants.

9. JOB TRAINING AND PARTNERSHIP ACT (1983)

The JTPA established a triangle partnership between business, labor, and government. This partnership would occur at all levels in order to deliver the maximum amount of training per dollar spent. The law targeted job training and related assistance to economically disadvantaged individuals, dislocated workers, and others who faced employment barriers such as these. The end goal was to turn trainees into full-time employees who could pull their own weight in the private sector and become productive members of the American work force.

10. FAMILY LEAVE ACT (1993)

We have President Bill Clinton to thank for this one. Under this act, employers must grant an eligible employee up to a total of twelve workweeks of unpaid leave during any twelve-month period. The reasons that such leave may be granted fall into the following categories: for the birth and care of an employee's newborn child; for placement with the employee of a son or daughter for adoption or foster care; care for an immediate family member such as a spouse, child, or parent with a serious health condition. In addition, an employee may take medical leave when the employee is unable to work because of a serious health condition.

Welcome to the Gilded Age

The Gilded Age in America gave way to the growth of industry and a substantial increase in immigration to America. This marked an important period in American history that was characterized by the production of iron and steel and the cultivation of western resources such as lumber, gold, and silver. In turn, such industrial activity sparked the demand for better transportation and promoted the growth and developments of railroads as they moved goods from the resource-rich West to the East. At this time, steel and oil were in great demand. Industrial development produced notable wealth for a number of businessmen like John D. Rockefeller (in oil) and Andrew Carnegie (in steel). Such titans were known as "robber barons," or those who got rich through ruthless business deals. The period was named the "Gilded Age" because of the many great fortunes created and the way of life this wealth supported during this period.[1]

1. FIRST PUBLIC DEMONSTRATION OF EDISON'S LIGHTBULB (DECEMBER 31, 1879)

The electric light we take for granted came to be on December 31, 1879. After toiling in his laboratory with thousands

[1] Information gathered from www.loc.gov.

of experiments, Edison demonstrated to the public the wonders of the first incandescent lightbulb at his laboratory in Menlo Park, New Jersey. This incandescent bulb has a thin filament that gives off light when heated to incandescence, when it becomes hot enough to emit light. An electric current provides the heat source.

2. FIRST LABOR DAY HOLIDAY CELEBRATED (SEPTEMBER 5, 1882)

The Labor Day that we know today signals the end of summer and the beginning of school. The very first Labor Day was held on Tuesday, September 5, 1882, in New York City. It was celebrated with a picnic, a concert, and speeches and was meant to be a respite from the daily toils of labor. Some ten thousand workers marched in a parade from New York's City Hall to Union Square. The day was designated a celebration that would be held each year on the first Monday in September. Soon after the first Labor Day, Congress passed legislation making Labor Day a national holiday in 1894.

3. WORLD'S FIRST HYDROELECTRIC POWER PLANT BEGINS OPERATION (SEPTEMBER 30, 1882)

Rushing waterfalls and rivers don't necessarily make you think of electricity, but hydroelectric power plants light our homes and neighborhoods. Using waterpower to drive power plants that produce electricity was the plan on September 30, 1882, when the world's first hydroelectric power plant began operation on the Fox River in Appleton, Wisconsin.

4. FIRST COCA-COLA SERVED (MAY 8, 1886)

Coca-Cola is one of the most recognized brand names throughout the world. People have been drinking the popular beverage since 1886, when an Atlanta pharmacist, John S. Pemberton, sold the first Coca-Cola at Jacob's Pharmacy in Atlanta, Georgia. Unbeknownst to many, it was actually bookkeeper Frank Robinson who came up with the product's now-famous name. It was also Robinson's handwriting of the name that would eventually come to be recognized as the famous Coca-Cola trademark.

5. ALEXANDER GRAHAM BELL INVENTS THE PHOTOPHONE (JUNE 3, 1880)

The Photophone was yet another invention that character-ized this time of ingenuity. Such a device was close to a solar-powered telephone and was invented by Alexander Graham Bell on June 3, 1880, some four years after he had patented the telephone. He considered the Photophone one of his most important inventions. The technology would rep-resent principles that would later be used in the technology that helps computers send information around the world today.

6. *GOOD HOUSEKEEPING* MAGAZINE INTRODUCED (MAY 2, 1885)

The magazine has been an American institution; however, the magazines displayed on the racks of early nineteenth century stores looked different than they do now. One maga-zine that was up front in the rack both then and now was *Good Housekeeping*. It first appeared on May 2, 1885, and offered readers tips for running a home, accompanied by stories and articles by expert writers and letters from readers. Clark W. Bryan was the magazine's first editor and described its early goal as being to "produce and perpetuate perfec-tion—or as near unto perfection as may be attained in the household."

7. FOUR STANDARD TIME ZONES FOR THE CONTINENTAL U.S. INTRODUCED (NOVEMBER 18, 1883)

As people increasingly became more mobile, they realized a need for the creation of time zones. In fact, at first the railroad managers tried to address the problem by establishing one hundred different railroad time zones. Soon, railroad sched-

uling became confusing and chaotic. It was the railway managers who finally agreed to use four time zones for the
continental United States: Eastern, Central, Mountain, and
Pacific. The railroads would no longer use local times. Today,
the U.S. Naval Observatory is responsible for establishing
the official time in the United States.

8. SUSAN B. ANTHONY SUPPORTS THE WOMEN'S SUFFRAGE AMENDMENT (MARCH 8, 1884)

In the days of old, a woman couldn't vote, but a man could.
The toil and persistence of some diligent activists won
women the right to vote. The brigade was lead by Susan B.
Anthony, and on March 8, 1884, Anthony testified before
Congress supporting women's suffrage, or their right to vote.
Anthony urged senators to support an amendment to the
U.S. Constitution that would enact this right. Such an
amendment, she said, "shall prohibit the disenfranchisement
of citizens of the United States on account of sex."

9. STATUE OF LIBERTY ARRIVES IN NEW YORK HARBOR (JUNE 19, 1885)

It was no easy task getting it here. A gift of international
friendship from France, the statue was disassembled into 350
pieces, packed in 214 crates, and transported to America.
Titled by its artist as "Liberty Enlightening the World," it was
reassembled about four months later on Bedloe's Island. On
October 28, 1886, President Grover Cleveland dedicated the
152-foot Statue of Liberty before thousands, not realizing
that millions more would come to know, meet, and love
"Lady Liberty."

10. THOMAS EDISON PATENTS THE KINETOSCOPE (AUGUST 31, 1887)

When Edison's assistant, W. K. L. Dickson, invented the motion picture, it turned out to be an immediate success. Edison thought that motion pictures were a toy creation, but he

hoped that they would boost sales of his record player and complement its use. He had a difficult time matching pictures with words. Therefore, he managed the creation of the kinetoscope—a device for viewing moving pictures without sound, and patented this invention on August 31, 1887.

It Makes the World
Go 'Round

Money—it's the substance of world commerce. We have come to understand money and currency as commonplace in our lives. When you really think about it, money is a medium of trust, as the paper of a five-dollar bill is worth no more than that of a one-hundred-dollar bill. Here are some interesting facts about money for you to ponder.

1. HISTORICALLY, IT HAS OFTEN BEEN FAKE

If you think U.S. currency has always been worth much more than the paper it's printed on, think again. In fact, by the end of the Civil War, nearly one-half of all U.S. paper currency in circulation was counterfeit. The U.S. Treasury Department created the U.S. Secret Service in 1865 to deal with such a problem. In less than a decade, the incidence of counterfeit currency was sharply reduced.

2. IT WAS ONCE BASED ON "ANTICIPATION"

Imagine modern–day government running on what it hopes it will pull down in revenue. Well, in 1775 American colonists issued paper currency for the Continental Congress to finance the Revolutionary War, which was backed by the "anticipation" of tax revenues. The notes were weak without solid backing and were easily counterfeited.

3.   IT HASN'T ALWAYS LOOKED THE SAME

Currency used to be about one-third greater in size than it currently is. In 1929 paper currency was reduced in size by 33 percent. It was also standardized, with uniform portraits on the faces of the currency and emblems and monuments on the backs.

4.   IT WASN'T ALWAYS THE U.S. DOLLAR

Most paper currency circulating between the Civil War and World War I consisted of national bank notes. Such notes were issued from 1863 through 1932 to increase the circulation of money in order to better meet the needs of business. From 1863 to 1877 private bank note companies under contract to the federal government printed national bank notes, until the government took over printing them in 1877.

5.   IT WASN'T ALWAYS "IN GOD WE TRUST"

The whole philosophy behind paper currency as a medium of exchange is based upon trust. The emphasis on trust wasn't enacted until 1955, when a law was passed under President Eisenhower that all new designs for coin and currency would bear the inscription "In God We Trust." But this wasn't the first time these words appeared on U.S. currency. They first appeared on the U.S. two-cent piece in 1864.

6.   PAPER CURRENCY HONORS MOSTLY MEN

Have you ever noticed this? Many women have appeared in some scenes on U.S. currency; however, only two historical women appear on American paper currency. If you look closely, you'll find that Martha Washington's portrait appears on the face of the 1886 and 1891 one-dollar silver certificate and on the back of the 1896 certificate. Further investigation will also show Pocahontas in the engraving "Introduction of the Old World to the New World," which is featured on several pieces of American paper currency.

7. FEW NATIVE AMERICANS ARE FOUND ON U.S. CURRENCY

Native Americans are very underrepresented on U.S. currency. In fact, Sioux Chief Running Antelope is the only Native American whose portrait is featured, on series 1899 silver certificates. His portrayal created a scandal, as the chief was shown in a Pawnee headdress rather than his Sioux tribal headdress. This also created additional friction between the Pawnee and the Sioux tribes. Pocahontas is also featured on U.S. currency; however, many other notable Native Americans are not.

8. U.S. CURRENCY ISN'T THE MOST WIDELY CIRCULATED CURRENCY

U.S. currency is the most widely circulated currency, right? Wrong! Rumor has it that the amount of play money for the Parker Brothers board game Monopoly exceeds the amount of money issued annually by the U.S. government. It's all in the game.

9. THE DOLLAR BILL IS RELATIVELY NEW

In our everyday world, people are trying to get rid of the penny, saying it takes up space and time and trouble as a currency medium where inflation creeps up each and every year. Well, if you think the dollar bill falls into the same category, you might be amazed to know that the one-dollar denomination of federal notes as it appears today first came off the press in 1963. Prior to that it had a different appearance and was actually backed by silver. Before 1957 it did not have "In God We Trust" printed on it. The two-dollar denomination was added in 1976. The one-hundred-dollar note has been the largest denomination printed since 1969.

10. A "CASHLESS SOCIETY" IS NOT LIKELY

Most everything seems to be electronic nowadays, so perhaps U.S. currency could be at the end of its useful life, right?

Wrong again! Predictions of a "cashless society" being over-taken by electronic payments are obscured by the fact that public demand for currency continues to grow. Credit and debit cards used for purchases may reduce the need for cash; however, paper currency still provides the advantage of privacy and will very likely continue its popularity for many years to come.

The Slide of Entitlements

S ocial Security and other governmental entitlement programs are among the most controversial issues in the
economic realm of our society. Politicians seem to be in a
never-ending debate about such programs. Employers and
citizens continually gripe about their high cost and their de-
clining benefit. It's interesting to see what past presidents
have said about Social Security and how . . . well, things just
keep getting worse. Below are ten quotations that illustrate
what ten presidents had to say about the topic.[1]

1. FRANKLIN DELANO ROOSEVELT (MESSAGE TO CONGRESS, JANUARY 17, 1935)

"In the important field of security for our old people, it seems
necessary to adopt three principles: First, non-contributory
old-age pensions for those who are now too old to build up
their own insurance. It is, of course, clear that for perhaps
thirty years to come funds will have to be provided by the
states and the federal government to meet these pensions.
Second, compulsory contributory annuities which in time

[1] Quotations excerpted from the Social Security Online Web site,
www.ssa.gov/history/presstmts.html. They have been edited for
style.

will establish a self-supporting system for those now young and for future generations. Third, voluntary contributory annuities by which individual initiative can increase the annual amounts received in old age. It is proposed that the federal government assume one-half of the cost of the old-age pension plan, which ought ultimately to be supplanted by self-supporting annuity plans."

2. HARRY TRUMAN (STATEMENT BY THE PRESIDENT ON THE 10TH ANNIVERSARY OF THE SOCIAL SECURITY ACT, AUGUST 13, 1945)

"A sound system of social security requires careful consideration and preparation. Social security worthy of the name is not a dole or a device for giving everybody something for nothing. True social security must consist of rights, which are earned rights—guaranteed by the law of the land. Only that kind of social security is worthy of the men and women who have fought and are now fighting to preserve the heritage and the future of America."

3. DWIGHT D. EISENHOWER (STATEMENT BY THE PRESIDENT CONCERNING THE NEED FOR A PRESIDENTIAL COMMISSION ON FEDERAL/STATE RELATIONS, FEBRUARY 26, 1953)

"The development of the federal Social Security system warrants study. This analysis should encompass not only the distribution of costs between the state and federal government but also the operation and coverage of the system itself. It is a proper function of government to help build a sturdy floor over the pit of personal disaster, and to this objective we are all committed. However, we are equally committed to carrying out that great program efficiently and with greatest benefit to those whom it is designed to help."

4. JOHN F. KENNEDY (SPECIAL MESSAGE TO THE CONGRESS ON PUBLIC WELFARE PROGRAMS, FEBRUARY 1, 1962)

"Our system of social insurance and related programs has grown greatly: in 1940 less than 1 percent of the aged were

receiving monthly old age insurance benefits; today over
two-thirds of our aged are receiving these benefits. In 1940
only 21,000 children, in families where the breadwinner had
died, were getting survivor insurance benefits; today such
monthly benefits are being paid to about 2 million children."

5. LYNDON JOHNSON (REMARKS WITH PRESIDENT TRUMAN AT THE SIGNING IN INDEPENDENCE OF THE MEDICARE BILL, JULY 30, 1965)

"No longer will older Americans be denied the healing mira-
cle of modern medicine. No longer will illness crush and destroy the savings that they have so carefully put away over a
lifetime so that they might enjoy dignity in their later years.
No longer will young families see their own incomes, and
their own hopes, eaten away simply because they are carrying out their deep moral obligations to their parents, and to
their uncles, and their aunts."

6. RICHARD NIXON (SPECIAL MESSAGE TO CONGRESS ON SOCIAL SECURITY, SEPTEMBER 25, 1969)

"By acting to raise benefits now to meet the rise in the cost
of living, we keep faith with today's recipients. By acting to
make future benefit raises automatic with rises in the cost of
living, we remove questions about future years; we do much
to remove this system from biennial politics; and we make
fair treatment of beneficiaries a matter of certainty rather
than a matter of hope."

7. GERALD FORD (REMARKS AT A MEETING WITH ADMINISTRATION OFFICIALS TO DISCUSS THE SOCIAL SECURITY TRUST FUND, MAY 6, 1976)

"As everybody knows, I submitted to the Congress a very
constructive proposal for the purpose of maintaining the financial integrity of the social security trust fund. This was

submitted at the time of our budget or economic program, at the time of the State of the Union and, unfortunately, it appears that the Congress is going to fail to recognize the problem and tragically fail to do anything to solve the problem."

8. JIMMY CARTER (REMARKS ON SIGNING H.R. 3 INTO LAW, OCTOBER 25, 1977)

"As most of you know, I was governor for four years and later spent two years campaigning around the country to be elected president. I think one of the greatest problems that we have in this nation is a distrust of government and its ability to administer programs of great benefit to our people in an honest and efficient way. Perhaps one of the most sensitive issues is in health care. We have seen the cost of a day's stay in the hospital increase since 1950 more than 1,000 percent. The cost of hospital care is going up a hundred percent, doubling every five years."

9. RONALD REAGAN (LETTER TO CONGRESSIONAL LEADERS ON THE SOCIAL SECURITY SYSTEM, MAY 21, 1981)

"As you know, the Social Security System is teetering on the edge of bankruptcy. Over the next five years, the Social Security trust fund could encounter deficits of up to $111 billion, and in the decades ahead its unfunded obligations could run well into the trillions. Unless we in government are willing to act, a sword of Damocles will soon hang over the welfare of millions of our citizens."

10. GEORGE W. BUSH (REMARKS BY THE PRESIDENT AT REPUBLICAN CONGRESSIONAL RETREAT, FEBRUARY 2, 2001)

"I believe I've got a limited amount of capital, and I'm going to spend it wisely and spend it in a focused way. One item is Social Security, another is Medicare reform. We have a fantastic opportunity to seize the initiatives to make sure that working with people like Chairman [William M.] Thomas, to make sure that the Medicare system works. Prescription drugs need to be an integral part of Medicare delivery system. It will be a proud moment for all of us, Republicans and Democrats, to say we came together to modernize Medicare so that the seniors can retire in dignity."

Blazing the Trail

Transportation is the lifeblood behind most of the goods, products, and people we come in contact with daily. Anything manufactured relies on transportation for finished goods movement as well as raw materials movement. Of course, people rely on transportation to do just about anything. But it hasn't always been so convenient and available. Here are ten events that shaped the current state of transportation in our nation as we know it today.

1. STEAM POWER

It was way up yonder on New York's Hudson River that Robert Fulton set off the first commercially successful steamboat service in 1807. By the middle of the century, ships crossing the oceans were also powered by steam, drastically reducing travel time. A five-week ocean journey in 1800 took about eighteen days once the steam engine was up and running. By the end of the century, the same journey took only five days. By the late nineteenth century, railroads driven by steam locomotives were responsible for the transport of millions of passengers and over 690 million tons of cargo.

2. **THE ERIE CANAL**

A canal can open up the paths of trade and travel. On October 26, 1825, the Erie Canal opened, providing transit by vessel between the East Coast of the United States and the Great Lakes region. This canal also stimulated trade, and subsequently growth, out of New York City, exchanging manufactured goods from the city and its surroundings with agricultural products from the Midwest.

3. **THE BALTIMORE & OHIO RAILROAD**

The Baltimore & Ohio Railroad was the flagship of chartered transportation. On February 28, 1827, it became the first U.S. railway chartered for commercial transportation of freight and passengers. Those who invested in the railroad were hopeful that Baltimore, which was second fiddle to New

Museum of American Financial History

The Erie Canal opened on October 26, 1825, providing a water route between the Great Lakes and the Hudson River, which helped make New York City the most important commercial port in the nation.

York in terms of trade, would surpass the city in the compe-
tion for Western trade. New York was benefiting from the
open gates of the Erie Canal at the time and was leading the
race of goods and people moved in an out of the area.

4. THE OPENING OF THE SUEZ CANAL

The Suez Canal was not built in a snap. It took about ten
years of hard work before the canal was opened on November 17, 1869. The canal was long, long, long, stretching
some 101 miles across Egypt's Isthmus of Suez, connecting
the Mediterranean Sea with the Indian Ocean. It is one of the
most traveled waterways in the world.

5. THE NAILING OF THE GOLDEN SPIKE

There was a giant spike driven into the ground at Promontory
Summit in Utah Territory in 1869. Members of the Union Pacific and the Central Pacific drove this spike, which symbol-
ized completion of the first transcontinental railroad. The
new railway joined the nation from coast to coast. It also reduced to just one week the duration of a trip that previously
took four or more months.

6. THE CREATION OF TIME ZONES IN THE UNITED STATES

When traveling by train, keeping track of the time change
became a serious problem. In fact, traveling to the East or to
the West meant that a person would have to change his or
her watch by one minute every twelve miles. Railroad operators recognized the need for a new time plan in order to offer
a train schedule that could create accurate arrival and depar-
ture times. On November 18, 1883, four standard time zones
were created in the United States.

7. THE WRIGHT BROTHERS AND THEIR EXPERIMENT

In 1903 Wilbur and Orville Wright piloted and monitored
their flying machine in Kill Devil Hills, North Carolina. The
first flight was commanded by Orville and lasted just twelve
seconds. By the end of the day, Wilbur traveled 852 feet into

the air and was able to soar for fifty-seven seconds. Thus, the uplift of a heavy machine that was commanded by a pilot changed transportation for us all.

8. THE MODEL T FORD

In 1903 Henry Ford created his automobile manufacturing empire with the motto "I will build a car for the great multitude." His 1908 Model T—aka the "Tin Lizzie" or the "Flivver"—was offered for $750 without a tonneau cover, $850 with one. Over the course of its nineteen years of manufacture, its price dropped to $280. Over 15.5 million Model Ts were sold in the United States from 1908 through 1927, making way for the new era of the Motor Age in America. What once was transportation only for the privileged class would eventually become transportation for the common man—"a car for the great multitude."

9. THE CREATION OF THE PANAMA CANAL

The Panama Canal was built between 1906 and 1914. When it opened for traffic, ships would pass through it for about fifty-one miles between the Atlantic and Pacific Ocean entrances. This eliminated the eight-thousand-nautical-mile trip around the choppy and dangerous waters of South America's Cape Horn. The duration of ocean transport was greatly shortened. Goods and imports were able to reach their destination faster and often at a lower total cost.

10. THE INTERSTATE HIGHWAY

The Federal Highway Act of 1938 states, "The Chief of the Bureau of Public Roads is hereby directed to investigate and make a report of his findings and recommend feasibility of building, and cost of, super highways not exceeding three in number, running in a general direction from the eastern to the western portion of the United States, and not exceeding three in number, running from the northern to the southern portion of the United States, including the feasibility of a toll system on such roads." This began the construction of interstate highways to connect the ends of the country. In 1952 the Federal-Aid Highway Act authorized $25 million for the interstate system, whereby federal funds would match fifty-fifty the contributions made by a given locality. Later, the Federal-Aid Highway Act of 1954 authorized $175 million for the interstate system, to be used on a sixty-forty matching ratio.

Family-Friendly Finesse

Employees don't just worry about their own hides. They also worry about those in their family and, as such, seek out a company that can provide benefits that their loved ones will enjoy. In this sense, some companies are family-friendly. Does being family-friendly pay dividends? It certainly does if you're the receiver of some of the valuable perks companies offer. But it pays dividends to the shareholders too—yes, you read that right—the shareholders. When Merrill Lynch studied the performance of some family-friendly firms during a period in the late 1990s, it found that their average stock price outperformed the market by about 25 percent.

So just who are these firms, and what do they offer? Well, there are many, but here's a sampling of ten family-friendly companies that take the load off their employees in several ways so that they can better attend to their spouses and children during their off-work hours.

1. KPMG CONSULTING (HQ: MCLEAN, VIRGINIA)

This consulting firm puts the issue of work and family right out on the table in many of its policies and decisions. The company touts its family-friendly environment as an integral part its business agenda. It welcomes discussion of the topic and even rewards senior management who engender the policies and consideration of a work–family life balance.

2. SAS (HQ: CARY, NORTH CAROLINA)

Well, the company's software and Enterprise Resource Planning (ERP) applications may have been the biggest headaches to implement over the years, but the firm makes the well-being of its employees and their families a high priority. At a time when benefits are growing in cost, the firm offers free child care staffed with certified and trained teachers who specialize in the Montessori method. The firm also offers free health care for its employees. What's more, the company serves nutritious gourmet food and allows employees to take home the leftovers! That's what I call friendly!

3. IBM (HQ: ARMONK, NEW YORK)

Well, Big Blue isn't just big on technology. It's also big on giving its employees some real benefits. It offers employees the option of working twenty to thirty hours per week during a six-month period so that they can tend to family matters. It also offers a two-hour lunch break during the workday to attend to personal business.

4. MERCK & CO., INC. (HQ: WHITEHOUSE STATION, NEW JERSEY)

This successful pharmaceutical company has pioneered many great inventions in the pharmaceutical field. It also does a pretty good job of thinking out of the box when it comes to its own employees. Need your oil changed? No problem if you work at Merck. It offers on-site auto service. Need to go home from a hard day at work and make dinner? No problem either. It also offers take-out meals from its food service.

5. HALLMARK CARDS, INC. (HQ: KANSAS CITY, MISSOURI)

The greeting card giant has been cultivating the fine art of expression, and it seems to walk the talk when it comes to its own employees. The company offers employees up to $5,000 for the cost of adoption. It offers a cadre of other benefits, including a referral program for child-care and elder-care programs. Some of its more innovative offerings include seminars on managing and coping with elder care and young dependents. It even runs programs and activities at its facilities during holiday periods and recess periods to which employees can bring their children while the parents are at work.

6. HEALTHWISE, INC. (HQ: BOISE, IDAHO)

If you work at this prestigious health information organization, you just may enjoy taking a company bicycle out for a ride. The company provides bicycles for a middle-of-the-day urge to hop on a bike and pedal around town to clear your head. It also offers a whopping three weeks of vacation during the first year of employment and 100 percent employer-paid health insurance benefits for its full-time and part-time employees.

7. AMERICAN MANAGEMENT SYSTEMS (HQ: FAIRFAX, VIRGINIA)

AMS offers employees flexible hours and a "Life Balance" program. This provides employees with private one-on-one consulting for issues of their work and their life. This may include stress management from any source—even if it's the result of a problem boss! It also may include other issues, such as personal finance. Employees may also exchange overtime hours for additional personal time off.

8. GENERAL MILLS (HQ: MINNEAPOLIS, MINNESOTA)

The company that championed the strategic Cheerios brand has also become a champion of the family-friendly workplace. When the two-year-old daughter of the company's CEO locked herself in the bathroom right before the executive was to make a business presentation to a security analyst, the spirit so moved him to highlight the importance of work-family obligations. The company offers flexibility in work schedules, on-site top-notch child care, and back-up child care when the employee's own plan falls through. If the antics of raising a family stress you out, the company has an answer for that too: yoga and exercise classes.

9. THE STANDING PARTNERSHIP (HQ: ST. LOUIS, MISSOURI)

This small public relations firm offers adoption assistance, maternity leaves, flex time, telecommuting, and tuition reimbursement. These are some generous benefits for a small business founded as recently as 1991. Unusually, the firm doesn't just offer maternity leave for new mothers. They also offer paternity leave for new fathers.

10. TEXAS INSTRUMENTS (HQ: DALLAS, TEXAS)

This high-tech company is right up there with the top shops in providing employees the best for their families. The perks include flexible work schedules, new mother rooms for nursing mothers, and even a concierge service for whatever errand you may have. If grocery shopping is your biggest hassle, this just may be the place for you. The firm offers an on-site grocery delivery service. They also offer reimbursement of up to $4,000 toward the costs of adoption.

Bibliography

BOOKS

Anzovin, Steven, and Janet Podell. *Famous First Facts, International Edition: A Record of First Happenings, Discoveries, and Inventions in World History.* New York: H. W. Wilson, 2000.

Axelrod, Karen, and Bruce Brumberg. *Watch It Made in the USA: A Visitor's Guide to the Companies That Make Your Favorite Products.* 3rd edition. New York: Avalon Travel, 2002.

Carruth, Gorton, and Eugene Ehrlich. *The Harper Book of American Quotations.* New York: Harper and Row, 1988.

Collins, James C., and Jerry I. Porras. *Built to Last: Successful Habits of Visionary Companies.* New York: Harper Collins, 2002.

Downes, John, and Jordan Elliot Goodman. *Barron's Dictionary of Finance and Investment Terms.* Woodbury, NY: Barron's, 1985.

Louis, David. *2201 Fascinating Facts.* Avenel, NJ: Ridge Press, 1983.

Merriam-Webster's Biographical Dictionary. Springfield, MA: Merriam-Webster, 1995.

Parietti, Jeff. *The Book of Truly Stupid Business Quotes*. New York: HarperPerennial Library, 1997.

SELECTED WEB SITES

About.com (http://www.about.com)

Anything Left-Handed (http://www.anythinglefthanded.co.uk)

Born to Motivate (http://www.borntomotivate.com)

Boy Scouts of America (http://www.scouting.org)

Brainy Quote (http://www.brainyquote.com)

Brunswick Corporation (http://www.brunswickbilliards.com)

Family Business Magazine (http://www.familybusinessmagazine.com)

Federal Trade Commission (http://www.ftc.gov)

Find A Grave (http://www.findagrave.com)

History Channel (http://www.historychannel.com)

Internal Revenue Service (http://www.irs.gov)

iVillage (http://www.ivillage.com)

Leadership Now (http://www.leadershipnow.com)

Library of Congress (http://www.loc.gov)

Marks Quotes (http://www.marksquotes.com)

Monopoly's Official Site (http://www.monopoly.com)

Occupational Safety and Health Administration (http://www.osha.gov)

Oldest Companies (http://www.cftech.com/BrainBank/CORPORATEADMINISTRATION/OldestCos.html)

Probabilities in the Game of Monopoly (http://www.tkcs-collins.com/truman/monopoly/monopoly.shtm)

The Quotations Page (http://www.quotationspage.com)

Schwab Learning Foundation (http://www.schwablearning.org)

Scripophily.com (http://www.scripophily.com)

Small Business Administration (http://www.sba.gov)

Smithsonian Institution (http://www.si.edu)

Spicy Quotes (http://www.spicyquotes.com)

Topher's Breakfast Cereal Character Guide (http://www.lavasurfer.com/cereal-guide.html)

Twain Quotes (http://www.twainquotes.com)

USA Freedom Corps (www.usafreedomcorps.gov)

U.S. Department of Commerce (http://www.doc.gov)

U.S. Department of Labor (http://www.dol.gov)

U.S. Department of the Treasury (http://www.treas.gov)

U.S. Military Academy (http://www.usma.edu)

United States Patent and Trademark Office (http://www.usp
    to.gov)

U.S. National Archives and Records Administration (http://
    www.nara.gov)

The White House/White House Fellows (http://www.white
    housefellows.gov)

Index

Numbers in *italic* refer to pages with illustrations